JOHNSON'S JUVENAL
LONDON AND
THE VANITY OF HUMAN WISHES

DITED WITH INTRODUCTION, NOTES, LATIN TEXTS AND TRANSLATIONS
By NIALL RUDD

BRISTOL CLASSICAL PRESS

Cover illustrations

Juvenal: an engraving of an imaginary portrait taken from Barten Holyday's
translation of Juvenal (1673)
Johnson: from a drawing after Sir Joshua Reynolds' famous portrait

Printed and bound in Great Britain
by Short Run Press Ltd., Exeter, Devon

First published in paperback only, 1981; new
impression, in hardback and paperback, 1988.

Bristol Classical Press
226 North Street
Bedminster
Bristol BS3 1JD

ISBN 0-906515-64-5 paperback
ISBN 0-86292-292-5 hardback

ADDENDA AND CORRIGENDA

London (Notes)

18   Read *Criticism.*

74   Read Midgley.

83   Read 82.

209   There has been fire insurance from at least 1667.

230   The modern sense was slowly making headway.

237   The Weald should also be taken into account.

The Vanity of Human Wishes (Notes)

214   Read Catherine I (not Catherine the Great).

291–2   Add: In 291–6 and 308–9 J. turns to Cicero, *De Senectute* 29, 38, 9, 70, 85, and 73. See *Notes and Queries,* March 1986, 59.

354   Rather the prayer seems good to the suppliant but actually carries dangers.

CONTENTS

PREFACE

This commentary calls for some apology. I am very much an amateur in eighteenth century literature; I have not inspected any manuscripts; and my knowledge of the period is largely based on secondary sources. Yet it may still be possible, I hope, to contribute something new from other directions. Reading these poems again over the last few years, I have asked a number of questions about sense and syntax which have not always been answered in the major editions. No doubt D. Nichol Smith and E. L. McAdam assumed that such elementary matters required no explanation; and perhaps at their level they were right. The admirable Penguin edition offers more help of this kind, but again (doubtless for reasons of space) several points which might puzzle the student are left without comment. In the present work, on the other hand, a sophisticated reader may find more assistance than he wants. I hope he will not feel insulted. These are difficult poems (especially the second); in fact there are several places, indicated in the notes, where the editor himself is not wholly confident of his interpretation.

In view of the decline in the teaching of Greek and Latin, there is also room, I believe, for a commentary which draws more attention to classical allusions and refers to other ancient passages which, perhaps only in a half-conscious way, entered into the making of the poems. Juvenal, naturally, is the most important source, and texts and translations of his third and tenth satires have been supplied; but other writers too, notably Herodotus and Horace, were often in Johnson's mind. To approach these famous poems from the direction of Greece and Rome may now appear eccentric; yet in a sense that was the path followed by Johnson himself.

The Oxford University Press has kindly allowed me to print Johnson's drafts. These documents throw light on his methods of composition and provide some insight into how the texts evolved. For a discussion of these matters the reader is referred to Moody (1).

I have received help from friends and colleagues on various points of detail. To mention them all by name would make this book appear more ambitious than it actually is. I must, however, record my gratitude to Dr J. D. Fleeman, not only for his published work on the two poems, but also for his generous help and advice. (It should not, of course, be assumed that he shares all my opinions.) The editors of this series made valuable comments on my draft, and persuaded me to refer more frequently to the poems of Oldham and Dryden. Other debts are acknowledged in the notes and bibliography.

INTRODUCTION

Samuel Johnson, the greatest English man of letters, was born in Lichfield (about 120 miles N.W. of London) on 18 September, 1709. As many accounts of his life are available, it will be enough to provide the following sign-posts:

1717-25	Attends Lichfield Grammar School
1726-28	Works in his father's bookshop in Lichfield
1728	Enters Pembroke College, Oxford
1729	Leaves Oxford without a degree
1730-33	In Lichfield, Market Bosworth, and Birmingham
1735	Marries Elizabeth Porter ('Tetty'), a widow of 46
	Opens a school in Lichfield
1737	Makes his way to London with David Garrick
1738	13 May publishes *London: A Poem.*

As *London* and *The Vanity of Human Wishes* are based on two of Juvenal's satires, something should be said about the Roman poet. *Decimus Iunius Iuvenalis* (born about A.D. 60; died some time after 130) came from Aquinum, a town about 80 miles S.E. of Rome. Very little is known of his life. He published his first book of satires (nos. 1-5) under Trajan about A.D. 110 and his fourth book (nos. 10-12) under Hadrian about 125. To judge from his work he experienced a good deal of frustration and disappointment, but the tradition that he spent some years in exile is not well supported.

After enjoying little success in his lifetime, Juvenal came into fashion in the fourth century, survived the vicissitudes of the dark ages, and began to attract interest again after the eleventh century.[1] The first printed edition appeared at Rome before the end of 1469.[2] Translations began in England with the version by Sir Robert Stapylton (1647), but this was easily surpassed by Dryden's brilliant rendering of five satires, including nos. 3 and 10, in 1693. Though Johnson was familiar with Dryden's work, he chose to write in a rather different tradition, namely that of imitation. This he called 'a kind of middle composition between translation and original design, which pleases when the thoughts are unexpectedly applicable and the parallels lucky'.[3] Speaking from memory, Johnson thought the

---

1 See Highet, chapters 28-32.
2 See C.F. Bühler, 'The Earliest Editions of Juvenal', *Studies in the Renaissance* 2 (1955) 84-95.
3 'Life of Pope' in *The Lives of the Poets*, ed. G.B. Hill, Oxford 1905, iii, 176. In Pope's early editions Horace's Latin was printed *en face* for purposes of reference, and where *London* came closest to Juvenal Johnson saw to it that the reader had the Latin lines before him. So reproducing the original in the present edition is not merely a pedantic exercise.

tradition had begun with Rochester and Oldham, but it can be seen in embryonic form as early as Wyatt (1503-42). The theory was enunciated by Denham and Cowley in the 1650's and applied in Cowley's 'The Country Mouse' (1663). Similar ideas were gaining ground in France, where Boileau published a collection of satires, based loosely on Horace and Juvenal, in 1666. The example of Cowley and Boileau was followed by Rochester and Oldham in the 1670's, and the latter's 'up-dated' version of Juvenal 3 supplied several hints for Johnson's *London*. Dryden expressed misgivings about imitation in the preface to his translation of Ovid's *Epistles* (1680), but at least four imitations of Juvenal appeared between 1683 and 1694, and Horace was even more popular. The greatest achievements in the genre, however, belonged to the next century. Between 1712 and 1714 Swift adapted two Horatian epistles and one satire; and Pope's wonderful *Imitations of Horace*, eleven in all, appeared in the five years preceding *London*.[4]

Johnson wisely decided to avoid Horace, but he took up the challenge by turning to Juvenal, a writer whom he knew in three different ways: through a direct study of the Latin text, through the translations and imitations mentioned above, and through the scholarly comments which had appeared in the major editions since the renaissance. In this mass of material he found two main conceptions of Juvenal. The first saw him as primarily a moralist, whose castigation of a decadent, pagan society made him acceptable to Christian readers. The second saw him chiefly as a wit, whose devastating and often indecent attacks could be savoured with malicious pleasure. Johnson was acknowledging both points of view when he described the peculiarity of Juvenal as 'a mixture of gaiety and stateliness, of pointed sentences [i.e. sharp and perceptive epigrams] and declamatory grandeur'.[5] The actual proportions of the mixture, whether because of theme, mood, or age, varied somewhat as between Satire 3 and Satire 10; and the reader will find an even wider variation in Johnson's response. But in any case it is clear from what has been said of Juvenal's place in the English tradition that Johnson had strong literary reasons for attempting his imitations.

He also had historical reasons. Like Pope, he was living in a period when the parallel between England and Rome (in social structure, institutions, and cultural outlook) could be exploited in a very striking way, so as to produce works which were both literary allusions and at the same time independent, eighteenth-century poems. More particularly, since, in the years 1737-38, Johnson was vehemently opposed to Walpole's government, he was all the more receptive to Juvenal's angry condemnation of vice and corruption in Roman public life. Admittedly Juvenal was not, properly speaking, a *political* satirist; he never advocated a return to the republican constitution; nor did he attack contemporary figures of any political

---

4 For an informative account of imitation in English poetry see Brooks.
5 'Life of Dryden' in *Lives*, ed. Hill (see n.3 above) i, 447.

importance. (What he did was to use the notorious dead as *exempla* of folly and wickedness.) Nevertheless, from the early seventeenth century, he was widely admired as the 'opposition satirist' *par excellence*, and Dryden was following a long tradition when he praised him as 'a zealous vindicator of Roman liberty'.[6]

We do not know exactly why Johnson was so hostile to Walpole. The satirist's 'Toryism' is hardly the answer; such labels are vague and unreliable, and in any case Walpole's most powerful critics were Whigs. More probably we should think of the influence exerted by Savage, Guthrie, Harry Hervey, and the writers of *The Craftsman*. From listening to these men, the young Johnson, 'embittered at his failures in the Midlands and still unsure of himself in Grub Street', was disposed to blame his misfortunes on 'the system'; and Walpole *was* the system.[7] Such personal factors also animated Johnson's reading of Juvenal. After all the privations he had known, he felt a profound affinity with the Roman poet who, more vividly than any other, had conveyed the sting of failure and poverty. As an illustration of this affinity one thinks first of the central section of *London*, with its massive line SLOW RISES WORTH BY POVERTY DEPRESS'D. But the same deep feelings lie behind his reflections on the scholar's life in *The Vanity of Human Wishes*. Mrs Piozzi tells how, when he read these lines to his friends at Streatham, 'he burst into a passion of tears'.[8]

For such reasons as these, which all shade into one another, Johnson went to work. Thanks to the investigations of two modern scholars,[9] we can now suggest with some confidence that he used the Delphin edition (Prateus, 1684) along with the notes of the variorum commentary (Schrevelius, 1684). He seems to have worked to a large extent from memory – an astonishing feat, even in that age. And he was so familiar with the two commentaries that he sometimes embodied their notes in his imitations.

Having finished the work by about the end of March, Johnson wrote to Edward Cave, publisher of the *Gentleman's Magazine*, ostensibly acting on behalf of a needy friend. He was confident, he said, that Cave would reward it 'in a different manner from a mercenary bookseller, who counts the lines he is to purchase and considers nothing but the bulk'. He went on to add the following offer: 'As I am sensible I have transcribed it very coarsely, which, after having altered it, I was obliged to do, I will, if you please to transmit the sheets from the press, correct it

---

6 'A Discourse Concerning the Original and Progress of Satire' in Dryden's *Essays*, ed. W. P. Ker, Oxford 1926, ii, 87. This view of Juvenal is well documented by H. D. Weinbrot, *Augustus Caesar in 'Augustan' England*, Princeton 1978, chap. 5. I attempted to show how unhistorical it was in *The Satires of Horace*, Cambridge 1966, 258-73.

7 For these ideas I am indebted to Greene, chap. 4, especially pp. 91 and 106.

8 Mrs Piozzi, *Anecdotes of the Late Samuel Johnson*, LL.D., 1786, 50.

9 See Bloom and Bloom (1).

for you, and take the trouble of altering any stroke of satire which you may dislike.' Cave accepted the poem, but suggested that the name of Robert Dodsley, a better-known publisher, should appear on the title page. Dodsley agreed and paid Johnson ten guineas for the copyright. As it happened, *London* was published on the same morning as Pope's *1738*, so that, as Boswell remarked, 'England had at once its Juvenal and Horace as poetical monitors'. Pope's reaction to *London* was, we are told, 'candid and liberal'. 'He requested Mr Richardson . . . to endeavour to find out who this new author was. Mr Richardson, after some inquiry, having informed him that he had discovered only that his name was Johnson, and that he was some obscure man, Pope said, "He will soon be *déterré*".'[10]

A comparison of *London* with Juvenal *Sat.* 3 shows that Johnson has expanded the opening scene, the first part of the speaker's diatribe, and the later picture of the countryside, whereas he has shortened the woes of poverty and the dangers of city life. The passages on foreign residents, and the two epilogues, are more or less equal.

1. Juvenal begins by relating Umbricius' decision to leave Rome for Cumae, an old Greek colony on the coast, now rather deserted. He approves of the decision, listing some of the hazards of Roman life. Finally he describes the scene just outside the Porta Capena (1-20). Johnson gives a longer list of hazards and significantly alters the poet's reflections at the point of departure (Greenwich); for while Juvenal contrasts the squalid area outside the Porta Capena with what it was like in the days of King Numa (and makes a characteristic joke about the pious gentleman's love-life), Johnson is more respectful in his nostalgia, recalling the great days of Elizabeth when England was powerful abroad and internally sound. In this way he adds a *political* dimension (1-30).

2. Umbricius claims that Rome is a place where social nonentities grow rich by following sordid occupations. What room is there for him? He cannot lie or cheat (21-57). Thales omits the element of class resentment but imports political comment, satirising treasonable speeches in parliament, the stage licensing act, Walpole's *Gazetteer*, and the dispensing of patronage (31-90).

3. Umbricius' picture of country life, though favourable, is far from idyllic. Phrases like 'learn to love your hoe', 'to regale a hundred Pythagoreans' (i.e. vegetarians), and 'to become the owner of one lizard' (a somewhat minute piece of livestock) keep enchantment at a safe distance. Thales' vision (210-23) is longer and altogether more idealized, e.g. 'There ev'ry bush with nature's music rings, / There ev'ry breeze bears health upon its wings'.

4. In Juvenal the poor man's indignities are described at greater length (126-89). Some of the complaints, however, would have struck Johnson as morally dubious, e.g. what use is there in paying one's morning respects to rich old ladies

10 The material in this paragraph comes from Boswell i, 121 and 128-9.

when a great magistrate has got there first? And how scandalous it is that an up-start can afford to seduce a Roman matron when a decent citizen can barely pay for a whore! Again, Juvenal's amusing and rather patronising description of a country festival (171-9) is omitted by Johnson, who expands instead the idea of migration found in Juvenal vv. 162-3. Even these lines of escapist yearning contain a thrust at the activities of Spain (173).

5. Rather surprisingly, Johnson declines to render Juvenal's marvellously vivid description of Rome's traffic (232-67) and the objects hurled from open windows (268-77). (Did he consider the subject-matter too low?) Also, in talking of nocturnal violence, he leaves out Juvenal's quotation of the young blade's abuse with its class contempt and race hatred (292-6). The more even tenor of Johnson's style is apparent in his rather limited variation of question, exclamation, and reported speech. The contrast can be seen by simply looking at the punctuation of Juvenal's text.

6. In Juvenal's section on foreigners (58-125) prejudice is evoked by the sarcastic use of Greek terms, Greek names, and Greek mythology, by the implication that the immigrants are so much refuse washed down by the river or blown in by the wind, and by the employment of sexual or excretory images to point a rhetorical climax. In this last respect Johnson is much less coarse (in spite of 'sewer', 'clap', and 'whore'). He also gives the passage a patriotic tone by complaining in sonorous and elevated style that the Englishman has abandoned his native virtues (99-106 and 117-22).

London as a whole is less cynical than its model. It conveys a strong desire for integrity in politics and social life, and calls for a foreign policy which will uphold ancient traditions of national greatness. The country's ills at home and abroad are naively ascribed to Walpole's corrupt and supine administration – an error which Johnson later confessed.[11] And the vision of rural life is decidedly rosy. One must remember, however, not just that *London* is a young man's poem, but that even in 1738 it reflected only the dominant mood of the writer, not his total view. In spite of its vileness, the city had many attractions. Johnson was happy to stay there, and he once remarked in a famous pronouncement that 'when a man is tired of London, he is tired of life'.[12]

The main stages in the next period of Johnson's life are as follows:

1739   Stays with Dr John Taylor at Ashbourne in Derbyshire
1740   Mortgages the family house in Lichfield
            Returns to London; works for the *Gentleman's Magazine*
1742   Assists in the preparation of James's *Medicinal Dictionary*
            Begins to catalogue the Harleian Library

11 See Hawkins, *Life of Johnson*, 514; Boswell i, 131.
12 Boswell iii, 178.

1743	Writes his *Account of the Life of Richard Savage*
1746	Undertakes to compile a *Dictionary of the English Language*
1748	November, completes *The Vanity of Human Wishes.*

The rest of Johnson's life, during which he became a national celebrity, does not come within the scope of this commentary. He died on 13 December 1784 and was buried in Westminster Abbey.

Boswell tells us that most, if not all, of *The Vanity of Human Wishes* was written at Hampstead, where Mrs Johnson had lodgings. 'The fervid rapidity with which it was produced is scarcely credible. I have heard him say that he composed seventy lines of it in one day, without putting one of them upon paper till they were finished. I remember when I once regretted to him that he had not given us more of Juvenal's satires, he said he probably should give more, for he had them all in his head; by which I understood that he had the originals and correspondent allusions floating in his mind, which he could, when he pleased, embody and render permanent without much labour. Some of them, however, he observed, were too gross for imitation.'[13]

Johnson sold the copyright to Dodsley for fifteen guineas, and it was published in January 1749.

Readers may find it instructive to make a detailed comparison with Juvenal's tenth satire. The main points are as follows:

Juvenal

1-53 (53)   Introduction: most prayers are misguided and, if answered, harmful; various 'blessings', including eloquence, strength, wealth, and political status; the contrasting attitudes of Heraclitus and Democritus.

54-113 (60)   Political power: the downfall of Tiberius' powerful minister, Sejanus.

114-32 (19)   Eloquence: the fate of Cicero and Demosthenes.

133-87 (55)   Military glory: how Hannibal, Alexander, and Xerxes ended their careers.

188-288 (101)   Long life: physical decay, mental decay, the deaths of friends and relatives; Nestor, Priam, and others.

289-345 (57)   Beauty: the moral and physical dangers threatening handsome young men; Silius and Messalina.

346-66 (21)   Conclusion: prayers for Stoic virtues do no harm, but are unnecessary.

Johnson

1-72 (72)   Introduction: mankind's follies are observed from a vantage-point above the earth; the known world now stretches from China to

13 Boswell i, 192-3.

Peru; abstract nouns take the place of people, giving more stately and inclusive generalisations; the idea of a deity who derives malicious amusement from human foolishness is evaded by substituting Vengeance for God; Democritus becomes a much more dignified figure.

73-134 (62)   Political power: the fall of Wolsey; Juvenal's vulgarity and jeering insults are replaced by melancholy reflection on the vanity and transience of power.

135-74 (40)   Learning: this section is expanded in a way which reflects the poet's own interest and experience; the *exempla* are briefly and respectfully mentioned; no attempt is made to reproduce Juvenal's liveliness and malice.

175-254 (80)   Military glory: Charles XII of Sweden, Xerxes, Charles Albert of Bavaria. Instead of sneering at these great leaders, Johnson ponders sadly on their futility.

255-318 (64)   Long life: Johnson is fully aware of the dreary absurdity of old age, but he shortens Juvenal's catalogue of afflictions; he omits his obscenity; and he does not harp with such merciless insistence on physical indignities.

319-42 (24)   Beauty: the dangers which threaten beautiful girls. Johnson again avoids Juvenal's obscenity; he develops no *exempla*; and he confines himself entirely to heterosexual follies and their cost.

343-68 (26)   Conclusion: a positive Christian affirmation, including the values of faith (363), hope (343) and love (361), none of which appears in Juvenal.

Boswell observed 'His *Vanity of Human Wishes* has less of common life, but more of a philosophical dignity than his *London*. More readers, therefore, will be delighted with the pointed spirit of *London*, than with the profound reflection of the *Vanity of Human Wishes*. Garrick, for instance, observed in his sprightly manner, with more vivacity than regard to just discrimination, as is usual with wits, "When Johnson lived much with the Herveys, and saw a good deal of what was passing in life, he wrote his *London*, which is lively and easy. When he became more retired, he gave us his *Vanity of Human Wishes*, which is as hard as Greek. Had he gone on to imitate another satire, it would have been as hard as Hebrew." But the *Vanity of Human Wishes* is, in the opinion of the best judges, as high an effort of ethic poetry as any language can show.'[14]

14 Boswell i, 193-4.

Text

For *London*, apart from a few very minor corrections, I have followed the text printed in Dodsley's *Collection of Poems* (1748) vol. 1. This was the basis of all texts, except that of 1750, for over thirty-five years. The 1750 edition was a quarto reprint of the uncorrected first edition of 1738 and has no independent value. According to James Boswell the younger, Johnson made a few notes and alterations on a copy (now lost) of this inferior edition, and Boswell transcribed these marginalia onto his own copy of the 1789 edition of the *Poetical Works*. Since five of Boswell's six explanatory notes and all four of his new variants (at 5, 131, 218, and 241) had already been incorporated in Hawkins' edition of the *Works* in 1787, it is usually assumed that Hawkins too had access to Johnson's notes. There are, in addition, three emendations in Hawkins (at 74, 122, and 251) which were not recorded by Boswell. Should these also be ascribed to Johnson? Some scholars are doubtful; some go further and question whether Boswell's variants really come from Johnson. Could they, perhaps, have originated with Hawkins? Those who wish to pursue these problems should consult Moody (2) 23 and 31-5. In the present edition I have mentioned these later readings in the notes but have not admitted them to the text. Even if they do come from Johnson himself, ten years are enough, one may think, for a poem to assume its final form. After that it should be immune to further tinkering on the part of its author. This somewhat arbitrary position is easier to sustain when, as here, the later variants are either trivial or inferior.

As for *The Vanity of Human Wishes*, I have adhered to Dodsley's text of 1755, except in a few matters of spelling and punctuation. Again James Boswell the younger recorded some variants. Ten were taken from the first edition of 1749; of the remaining six (at 41, 138, 167, 268, 293, and 298), five had already appeared in Hawkins. Four other, rather feeble, emendations in Hawkins (at 199, 250, 340, and 348) were not recorded by Boswell. This time Boswell does not state explicitly that he is transcribing Johnson's handwriting, but in three instances (268, 293, and 298) he does add the words 'corr MSS' after the variant. For details the reader is referred to Moody (2) 24-30. Once again I have mentioned all these cases in the notes but have not printed them in the text.

Except in proper names, capitals are used only in clear instances of personification. There are, admittedly, doubtful cases, but it seemed better to attempt some distinction than to print every noun with a capital – a practice which tends to distract the modern reader without conveying any appreciable nuance.

The figures in square brackets in the left hand margin are intended to serve as a guide to the corresponding sections in Juvenal.

BIBLIOGRAPHY

The following works have been particularly useful to the editor in preparing the present commentary.

JOHNSON

Editions
Fleeman, J. D., *Samuel Johnson: the Complete English Poems*, Penguin Books 1971
McAdam, E. L. and Milne, G., *The Works of Samuel Johnson*, vol. 6, Yale 1964
Nichol Smith, D. and McAdam, E. L., *The Poems of Samuel Johnson*, 2nd ed. revised by
   J. D. Fleeman, Oxford 1974

Books
Bate, W. J., (1) *The Achievement of Samuel Johnson*, New York 1955
— (2) *Samuel Johnson*, London 1978
Boswell, J., *Life of Johnson*, ed. G. B. Hill, revised by L. F. Powell, Oxford 1934
   and 1950
Clifford, J. L., (1) *Young Sam Johnson*, New York 1955
— (2) *Dictionary Johnson*, London 1979
Greene, D. J., *The Politics of Samuel Johnson*, New Haven 1960
Wain, J., *Samuel Johnson*, 2nd ed. London 1980

Articles
Bloom, E. L. and Bloom, L. D., (1) 'Johnson's *London* and its Juvenalian Texts' and
   'Johnson's *London* and the Tools of Scholarship', *Huntington Library Quarterly* 24
   (1970-71) 1-23, 115-39
— — (2) 'Johnson's "Mournful Narrative": the Rhetoric of *London*', *Eighteenth
   Century Studies in Honor of Donald F. Hyde*, ed. W. H. Bond, New York 1970, 107-44
Brooks, H. F., 'The Imitation in English Poetry', *Review of English Studies* 25 (1949)
   124-40
Gifford, H., 'The Vanity of Human Wishes', *Review of English Studies* 6 (1955) 157-65
Humphreys, A. R., 'Johnson', *The Pelican Guide to English Literature* 4, From Dryden to
   Johnson, ed. Boris Ford, Penguin Books, repr. 1975
Moody, A. D., (1) 'The Creative Critic: Johnson's Revisions of *London* and *The Vanity of
   Human Wishes*', *Review of English Studies* 22 (1971) 137-50
— (2) 'Johnson's Poems: Textual Problems and Critical Readings', *The Library* 26
   (1971) 22-38
Needham, J. D., '*The Vanity of Human Wishes* as Tragic Poetry', *Australasian Universities
   Modern Language Association* 46 (1976) 206-19
Weinbrot, H. D., *The Formal Strain*, Chicago 1969, chaps. 7 and 8

Historical Background
George, M. D., *London Life in the Eighteenth Century*, London 1925
Grant Robertson, C., *England Under the Hanoverians*, London 1911
Kramnik, I., *Bolingbroke and his Circle*, Harvard 1968
Plumb, J. H., *The First Four Georges*, London 1961
Turberville, A. S. (Ed.), *Johnson's England*, 2 vols., Oxford 1933
Williams, B., *The Whig Supremacy*, 2nd ed. revised by C. H. Stuart, Oxford 1962

JUVENAL

Text
Clausen, W. V., *A. Persi Flacci et D. Iuni Iuuenalis Saturae*, Oxonii 1966

Commentaries
Courtney, E., *A Commentary on the Satires of Juvenal*, London and Indiana 1980
Duff, J. D., *D. Iunii Iuvenalis, Saturae XIV*, with new introduction by M. Coffey, Cambridge 1970

Translations
Green, P., *Juvenal: The Sixteen Satires*, Penguin Books 1967
Ramsay, G. G., *Juvenal and Persius*, Loeb Classical Library 1918

Book
Highet, G., *Juvenal the Satirist*, Oxford 1954

Articles
Eichholz, D. E., 'The Art of Juvenal and his Tenth Satire', *Greece and Rome* n.s.3 (1956) 61-9
Mason H. A., 'Is Juvenal a Classic?' *Critical Essays on Roman Literature*, ed. J. P. Sullivan, London 1963

LONDON

Quis ineptae
Tam patiens urbis, tam ferreus ut teneat se?

[1]   Tho' grief and fondness in my breast rebel,
When injur'd Thales bids the town farewell,
Yet still my calmer thoughts his choice commend,
I praise the hermit, but regret the friend,
Who now resolves, from vice and London far,
To breathe in distant fields a purer air,
And fix'd on Cambria's solitary shore,
Give to St. David one true Briton more.
    For who would leave, unbrib'd, Hibernia's land,
Or change the rocks of Scotland for the Strand?   10
There none are swept by sudden fate away,
But all whom hunger spares, with age decay:
Here malice, rapine, accident, conspire,
And now a rabble rages, now a fire;
Their ambush here relentless ruffians lay,
And here the fell attorney prowls for prey;
Here falling houses thunder on your head,
And here a female atheist talks you dead.
While Thales waits the wherry that contains
Of dissipated wealth the small remains,   20
On Thames's banks, in silent thought we stood,
Where Greenwich smiles upon the silver flood:
Struck with the seat that gave Eliza birth,
We kneel, and kiss the consecrated earth;
In pleasing dreams the blissful age renew,
And call Britannia's glories back to view;
Behold her cross triumphant on the main,
The guard of commerce, and the dread of Spain,
Ere masquerades debauch'd, excise oppress'd,
Or English honour grew a standing jest.   30
    A transient calm the happy scenes bestow,
And for a moment lull the sense of woe.
At length awaking, with contemptuous frown,
Indignant Thales eyes the neighb'ring town.

[21]   Since worth, he cries, in these degen'rate days,
Wants ev'n the cheap reward of empty praise;

In those curs'd walls, devote to vice and gain,
Since unrewarded science toils in vain;
Since hope but sooths to double my distress,
And ev'ry moment leaves my little less;   40
While yet my steady steps no staff sustains,
And life still vig'rous revels in my veins;
Grant me, kind heaven, to find some happier place,
Where honesty and sense are no disgrace;
Some pleasing bank where verdant osiers play,
Some peaceful vale with nature's paintings gay;
Where once the harrass'd Briton found repose,
And safe in poverty defy'd his foes;
Some secret cell, ye pow'rs, indulgent give.
Let —— live here, for —— has learn'd to live.   50
Here let those reign, whom pensions can incite
To vote a patriot black, a courtier white;
Explain their country's dear-bought rights away,
And plead for pirates in the face of day;
With slavish tenets taint our poison'd youth,
And lend a lye the confidence of truth.
    Let such raise palaces, and manors buy,
Collect a tax, or farm a lottery,
With warbling eunuchs fill a licens'd stage,
And lull to servitude a thoughtless age.   60
    Heroes, proceed! What bounds your pride shall hold?
What check restrain your thirst of pow'r and gold?
Behold rebellious virtue quite o'erthrown,
Behold our fame, our wealth, our lives your own.
    To such, a groaning nation's spoils are giv'n,
When publick crimes inflame the wrath of heav'n:
But what, my friend, what hope remains for me,
Who start at theft, and blush at perjury?
Who scarce forbear, tho' Britain's Court he sing,
To pluck a titled poet's borrow'd wing;   70
A statesman's logick unconvinc'd can hear,
And dare to slumber o'er the Gazetteer;
Despise a fool in half his pension dress'd,
And strive in vain to laugh at H——y's jest.
    Others with softer smiles, and subtler art,
Can sap the principles, or taint the heart;
With more address a lover's note convey,

Or bribe a virgin's innocence away.
Well may they rise, while I, whose rustick tongue
Ne'er knew to puzzle right, or varnish wrong,   80
Spurn'd as a beggar, dreaded as a spy,
Live unregarded, unlamented die.
   For what but social guilt the friend endears?
Who shares Orgilio's crimes, his fortune shares.
But thou, should tempting villainy present
All Marlb'rough hoarded, or all Villiers spent,
Turn from the glitt'ring bribe thy scornful eye,
Nor sell for gold, what gold could never buy,
The peaceful slumber, self-approving day,
Unsullied fame, and conscience ever gay.   90

[58]   The cheated nation's happy fav'rites, see!
Mark whom the great caress, who frown on me!
London! the needy villain's gen'ral home,
The common shore of Paris and of Rome,
With eager thirst, by folly or by fate,
Sucks in the dregs of each corrupted state.
Forgive my transports on a theme like this,
I cannot bear a French metropolis.
   Illustrious Edward! from the realms of day,
The land of heroes and of saints survey;   100
Nor hope the British lineaments to trace,
The rustick grandeur, or the surly grace,
But lost in thoughtless ease, and empty show,
Behold the warrior dwindled to a beau;
Sense, freedom, piety, refin'd away,
Of France the mimick, and of Spain the prey.
   All that at home no more can beg or steal,
Or like a gibbet better than a wheel;
Hiss'd from the stage, or hooted from the court,
Their air, their dress, their politicks import;   110
Obsequious, artful, voluble and gay,
On Britain's fond credulity they prey.
No gainful trade their industry can 'scape,
They sing, they dance, clean shoes, or cure a clap;
All sciences a fasting Monsieur knows,
And bid him go to hell, to hell he goes.

Ah! what avails it, that, from slav'ry far,
I drew the breath of life in English air;
Was early taught a Briton's right to prize,
And lisp the tale of Henry's victories;   120
If the gull'd conqueror receives the chain,
And flattery subdues when arms are vain?
 Studious to please, and ready to submit,
The supple Gaul was born a parasite:
Still to his int'rest true, where'er he goes,
Wit, brav'ry, worth, his lavish tongue bestows;
In ev'ry face a thousand graces shine,
From ev'ry tongue flows harmony divine.
These arts in vain our rugged natives try,
Strain out with fault'ring diffidence a lye,   130
And gain a kick for awkward flattery.
 Besides, with justice, this discerning age
Admires their wond'rous talents for the stage:
Well may they venture on the mimick's art,
Who play from morn to night a borrow'd part;
Practis'd their master's notions to embrace,
Repeat his maxims, and reflect his face;
With ev'ry wild absurdity comply,
And view each object with another's eye;
To shake with laughter ere the jest they hear, 140
To pour at will the counterfeited tear,
And as their patron hints the cold or heat,
To shake in dog-days, in December sweat.
 How, when competitors like these contend,
Can surly virtue hope to fix a friend?
Slaves that with serious impudence beguile,
And lye without a blush, without a smile;
Exalt each trifle, ev'ry vice adore,
Your taste in snuff, your judgment in a whore;
Can Balbo's eloquence applaud, and swear   150
He gropes his breeches with a monarch's air.
 For arts like these preferr'd, admir'd, caress'd,
They first invade your table, then your breast;
Explore your secrets with insidious art,
Watch the weak hour, and ransack all the heart;
Then soon your ill-plac'd confidence repay,
Commence your lords, and govern or betray.

[126]   By numbers here from shame or censure free,
          All crimes are safe, but hated poverty.
          This, only this, the rigid law pursues,   160
          This, only this, provokes the snarling muse.
          The sober trader at a tatter'd cloak,
          Wakes from his dream, and labours for a joke;
          With brisker air the silken courtiers gaze,
          And turn the varied taunt a thousand ways.
          Of all the griefs that harrass the distress'd,
          Sure the most bitter is a scornful jest;
          Fate never wounds more deep the gen'rous heart,
          Than when a blockhead's insult points the dart.
              Has heaven reserv'd, in pity to the poor,   170
          No pathless waste, or undiscover'd shore?
          No secret island in the boundless main?
          No peaceful desart yet unclaim'd by Spain?
          Quick let us rise, the happy seats explore,
          And bear oppression's insolence no more.
          This mournful truth is ev'ry where confess'd,
          SLOW RISES WORTH, BY POVERTY DEPRESS'D:
          But here more slow, where all are slaves to gold,
          Where looks are merchandise, and smiles are sold,
          Where won by bribes, by flatteries implor'd,   180
          The groom retails the favours of his lord.

[190]   But hark! th'affrighted crowd's tumultuous cries
          Roll thro' the streets, and thunder to the skies;
          Rais'd from some pleasing dream of wealth and pow'r,
          Some pompous palace, or some blissful bow'r,
          Aghast you start, and scarce with aking sight
          Sustain th'approaching fire's tremendous light;
          Swift from pursuing horrors take your way,
          And leave your little ALL to flames a prey;
          Then thro' the world a wretched vagrant roam,   190
          For where can starving merit find a home?
          In vain your mournful narrative disclose,
          While all neglect, and most insult your woes.
              Should heaven's just bolts Orgilio's wealth confound,
          And spread his flaming palace on the ground,
          Swift o'er the land the dismal rumour flies,
          And publick mournings pacify the skies;

The laureat tribe in servile verse relate,
How Virtue wars with persecuting Fate;
With well-feign'd gratitude the pension'd band   200
Refund the plunder of the beggar'd land.
See! while he builds, the gaudy vassals come,
And crowd with sudden wealth the rising dome;
The price of boroughs and of souls restore,
And raise his treasures higher than before.
Now bless'd with all the baubles of the great,
The polish'd marble, and the shining plate,
Orgilio sees the golden pile aspire,
And hopes from angry heav'n another fire.

    Could'st thou resign the park and play content,   210
For the fair banks of Severn or of Trent;
There might'st thou find some elegant retreat,
Some hireling senator's deserted seat;
And stretch thy prospects o'er the smiling land,
For less than rent the dungeons of the Strand;
There prune thy walks, support thy drooping flow'rs,
Direct thy rivulets, and twine thy bow'rs;
And, while thy beds a cheap repast afford,
Despise the dainties of a venal lord:
There ev'ry bush with nature's musick rings,   220
There ev'ry breeze bears health upon its wings;
On all thy hours security shall smile,
And bless thine evening walk and morning toil.

[268]   Prepare for death, if here at night you roam,
And sign your will before you sup from home.
Some fiery fop, with new commission vain,
Who sleeps on brambles till he kills his man;
Some frolick drunkard, reeling from a feast,
Provokes a broil, and stabs you for a jest.
Yet ev'n these heroes, mischievously gay,   230
Lords of the street, and terrors of the way;
Flush'd as they are with folly, youth and wine,
Their prudent insults to the poor confine;
Afar they mark the flambeau's bright approach,
And shun the shining train, and golden coach.
    In vain, these dangers past, your doors you close,
And hope the balmy blessings of repose:

Cruel with guilt, and daring with despair,
The midnight murd'rer bursts the faithless bar;
Invades the sacred hour of silent rest,   240
And plants, unseen, a dagger in your breast.

   Scarce can our fields, such crowds at Tyburn die,
With hemp the gallows and the fleet supply.
Propose your schemes, ye senatorian band,
Whose Ways and Means support the sinking land;
Lest ropes be wanting in the tempting spring,
To rig another convoy for the k——g.

   A single jail, in Alfred's golden reign,
Could half the nation's criminals contain;
Fair Justice then, without constraint ador'd,   250
Held high the steady scale, but deep'd the sword;
No spies were paid, no special juries known,
Blest age! but ah! how diff'rent from our own!

[315]   Much could I add, – but see the boat at hand,
The tide retiring, calls me from the land:
Farewell! – When youth, and health, and fortune spent,
Thou fly'st for refuge to the wilds of Kent;
And tir'd like me with follies and with crimes,
In angry numbers warn'st succeeding times;
Then shall thy friend, nor thou refuse his aid,   260
Still foe to vice, forsake his Cambrian shade;
In virtue's cause once more exert his rage,
Thy satire point, and animate thy page.

JUVENAL, SATIRE 3

Although upset by my old friend's departure, nevertheless I approve of his decision to make his home in empty Cumae [a ghost town near Naples] and to present the Sibyl with one fellow-citizen. It is the gateway to Baiae [a fashionable resort], and a delightful stretch of coast offering beauty and seclusion. For myself, I prefer even Prochyta [a small island off Cape Misenum] to the Subura [Rome's Soho]; for where have we ever seen a place so run down and so lonely that one would not think it worse to live in fear of continual fires and falling houses and the hundred and one dangers of this savage city, including poets reciting in the month of August?

(10) But while his entire household was being loaded onto a single waggon, he stopped at the damp old archway of the Porta Capena. At this point, where King Numa used to meet his nocturnal girl-friend [the nymph Egeria], and where now the grove with its holy spring and shrine is leased to Jews, whose paraphernalia amount to a haybox (every tree is obliged to pay rent to the public; the Muses have been evicted and the wood has taken to begging), we go down to the valley of Egeria and to a grotto unlike the real thing. How much better would the spirit of the spring be if a bank of green grass surrounded the water and no marble clashed with the native tufa!

(21) Here then Umbritius began to speak. 'Since,' he said, 'there is no room in the city for respectable occupations, and no return for honest work, and since my assets today are less than they were yesterday, and tomorrow there will be further attrition of the little that remains, I intend to go to the place where Daedalus took off his weary wings, while my white hairs are just beginning, while my old age is not far advanced and still has a straight back, while Lachesis [one of the three Fates] has something left to spin and I can support myself on my own two feet without leaning my hand on a walking stick. Let me say goodbye to my native district. (29) Let Arturius and Catulus live there; let those stay behind who turn black into white, who readily accept contracts for temple, river, and

JUVENAL, SATIRE 3

Quamvis digressu veteris confusus amici,
Laudo tamen vacuis quod sedem figere Cumis
Destinet, atque unum civem donare Sibyllae.
Janua Baiarum est, & gratum littus amoeni
Secessus. Ego vel Prochytam praepono Suburrae.
Nam quid tam miserum & tam solum vidimus, ut non
Deterius credas horrere incendia, lapsus
Tectorum assiduos, ac mille pericula saevae
Urbis, & Augusto recitantes mense poetas?
Sed dum tota domus rheda componitur una,   10
Substitit ad veteres arcus, madidamque Capenam;
Hic ubi nocturnae Numa constituebat amicae,
Nunc sacri fontis nemus & delubra locantur
Judaeis, quorum cophinus foenumque supellex;
Omnis enim populo mercedem pendere jussa est
Arbor, & ejectis mendicat silva Camoenis,
In vallem Aegeriae descendimus & speluncas
Dissimiles veris. Quanto praestantius esset
Numen aquae, viridi si margine clauderet undas
Herba, nec ingenuum violarent marmora tophum?   20

    Hic tunc Umbritius; Quando artibus, inquit, honestis
Nullus in urbe locus, nulla emolumenta laborum,
Res hodie minor est here quam fuit atque eadem cras
Deteret exiguis aliquid; proponimus illuc
Ire fatigatas ubi Daedalus exuit alas;
Dum nova canities, dum prima & recta senectus,
Dum superest Lachesi quod torqueat & pedibus me
Porto meis, nullo dextram subeunte bacillo.
Cedamus patria; vivant Arturius istic,
Et Catulus: maneant qui nigra in candida vertunt,   30
Queis facile est aedem conducere, flumina, portus,

harbour, for draining floods, and for carrying corpses to the pyre, and who put themselves up for auction under the shadow of the spear [i.e. have themselves declared bankrupt to evade their debts]. These were once hornplayers, always to be seen at provincial arenas, their cheeks known in every country town. Now they *present* shows, and when the crowd turns up its thumb they kill anyone at all to tumultuous applause. Then they come home and hire out latrines. And why stop at anything? For they are the sort that Lady Luck raises from the gutter to the pinnacle of power when she feels like enjoying a joke.

(41) What could I do in Rome? I can't tell lies; if a book is bad I can't praise it and ask for a copy; I know nothing of the stars' movements; I'm neither willing nor able to promise the death of someone's father; I've never studied frogs' innards [as a means of augury]; I leave it to others to carry an adulterer's presents and messages to a married woman; I will not be a thief's henchman, and for that reason no governor takes me on his staff; it's as if I were maimed – a useless trunk with mutilated hands. Who now is treated with affection unless he's an accomplice and his heart boils and seethes with unmentionable secrets? (51) If a man lets you into an honourable secret he doesn't think he is in your debt and he will never buy your silence. But that man will be dear to Verres [a crooked governor of Sicily] who can prosecute Verres whenever he likes. All the sand of shady Tagus and all the gold that it carries down to the sea would never make it worth while for you to lose your sleep, to accept uneasily gifts which ought to be turned down, and always to be an object of fear to your powerful friend.

I move quickly on to speak of the nation which is most highly prized by our wealthy citizens and which I abominate above all others; and no embarrassment will prevent me. Romans, I cannot bear a Greek capital. (61) And yet how small a fraction of the rabble is from Greece proper [as distinct from the Greek-speaking areas of the E. Mediterranean]? The Syrian Orontes has long been discharging into the Tiber, carrying with it its language and ways of behaviour, its slanting strings (with piper's accompaniment), its native tambourines, and its girls who have been instructed to ply their trade at the Circus [i.e. outside the racetrack]. (If you fancy a foreign whore in a coloured bonnet, that's the place to go.) Your country lad, Romulus, puts on his dinner-shoes (à la grecque) and wears medals (à la grecque) on his neck which is smudged with mud from the wrestling floor (à la grecque). Here's a fellow from high-perched Sicyon, that one's from far off Amydon, another's from Andros or Samos or Tralles or Alabanda. They make for the Esquiline and the hill named after the willow [the

Siccandam eluviem, portandum ad busta cadaver,
Et praebere caput domina venale sub hasta.
Quondam hi cornicines & municipalis arenae
Perpetui comites, notaeque per oppida buccae,
Munera nunc edunt, & verso pollice vulgi
Quemlibet occidunt populariter: inde reversi
Conducunt foricas. Et cur non omnia? Cum sint
Quales ex humili magna ad fastigia rerum
Extollit, quoties voluit Fortuna jocari.   40
Quid Romae faciam? Mentiri nescio, librum,
Si malus est, nequeo laudare & poscere: motus
Astrorum ignoro: funus promittere patris
Nec volo, nec possum: ranarum viscera nunquam
Inspexi: ferre ad nuptam quae mittit adulter,
Quae mandat, norint alii; me nemo ministro
Fur erit: atque ideo nulli comes exeo, tanquam
Mancus & extinctae corpus non utile dextrae.
Quis nunc diligitur, nisi conscius & cui fervens
Aestuat occultis animus, semperque tacendis?   50
Nil tibi se debere putat, nil conferet unquam,
Participem qui te secreti fecit honesti.
Carus erit Verri, qui Verrem tempore, quo vult,
Accusare potest. Tanti tibi non sit opaci
Omnis arena Tagi, quodque in mare volvitur aurum,
Ut somno careas, ponendaque praemia sumas
Tristis & a magno semper timearis amico.

Quae nunc divitibus gens acceptissima nostris,
Et quos praecipue fugiam, properabo fateri;
Nec pudor obstabit. Non possum ferre, Quirites,   60
Graecam urbem; quamvis quota portio faecis Achaeae?
Jampridem Syrus in Tiberim defluxit Orontes,
Et linguam & mores & cum tibicine chordas
Obliquas, necnon gentilia tympana secum
Vexit & ad Circum jussas prostare puellas.
Ite, quibus grata est picta lupa barbara mitra.
Rusticus ille tuus sumɪt trechedipna, Quirine,
Et ceromatico fert niceteria collo.
Hic alta Sicyone, ast hic Amydone relicta,
Hic Andro, ille Samo, hic Trallibus, aut Alabandis,   70
Esquilias, dictumque petunt a vimine collem,

Viminal], all set to be the vital organs of the great houses and to become their masters. (73) Nimble wits, shameless impudence, a ready tongue more fast-flowing than Isaeus' [an Assyrian teacher of rhetoric]. Tell me, what do you think he is? He has brought to us in his own person every man you can think of. Grammarian, rhetorician, geometrician, painter, masseur, augur, tightrope walker, doctor, sorcerer – he knows the lot. If you order him to mount to the skies, your hungry little Greek will go. In fact the man who grew wings [Daedalus] was no Moor, Sarmatian, or Thracian, but one born in the centre of Athens. (81) Shall I not get away from their purple clothes (à la grecque)? Is that fellow to append his signature [as a witness] before me? And is he to recline at dinner in a higher place than mine – someone who was blown to Rome by the wind which brought damsons and figs? Is it of such total unimportance that my infancy drew in the air of the Aventine and was nourished on the Sabine berry [the olive]? What of the fact that the nation is expert in flattery, praises the speech of an inarticulate patron and the looks of an ugly one, and compares the stalk-like neck of a weakling to the bull neck of Hercules as he holds Antaeus [an earth-born African giant] off the ground? (90) He exclaims in admiration at a squeaky voice as wretched as that of the husband when he bites his partner in the hen-run. We too can praise such things, but they are believed. Is any comic actor better when he plays Thais [the courtesan], or the wife, or Doris [the servant girl] who wears only a tunic? Why the woman herself seems to be speaking, not an actor. You'd swear that everything below her tummy was flat and even, divided by a tiny chink. And yet over there Antiochus would not be thought exceptional, nor Stratocles, nor Demetrius with his dainty friend Haemus. The whole country's a cast. (100) You chuckle? He shakes with a loud guffaw. If he sees a tear in his patron's eye, he weeps – yet he feels no grief. If you ask for a brazier in mid winter, he puts on a heavy wrap. If you say 'I'm warm', he breaks into a sweat. So we aren't on equal terms. He has the best of it, being able on all occasions, night or day, to put on another man's face, ready to gesticulate in keeping with his expression, and to praise his patron for a fine belch, a good straight pee, or for making the golden receptacle [i.e. an expensive commode] clatter as its bottom turns upside down. (109) Moreover, nothing is sacrosanct or safe from his organ – not the lady of the house, nor her virgin daughter, not even her still beardless future son-in-law, nor her hitherto clean-living son. If none of these is available, he turns his patron's house upside down. They want to find out the household's secrets and, as a re-

Viscera magnarum domuum, dominique futuri.
Ingenium velox, audacia perdita, sermo
Promptus & Isaeo torrentior: ede quid illum
Esse putes. Quemvis hominem secum attulit ad nos.
Grammaticus, Rhetor, Geometres, Pictor, Aliptes,
Augur, Schoenobates, Medicus, Magus: omnia novit.
Graeculus esuriens, in coelum jusseris, ibit.
Ad summam non Maurus erat, nec Sarmata, nec Thrax,
Qui sumpsit pennas, mediis sed natus Athenis.   80
Horum ego non fugiam conchylia? Me prior ille
Signabit? Fultusque toro meliore recumbet
Advectus Romam, quo pruna & coctona vento?
Usque adeo nihil est, quod nostra infantia coelum
Hausit Aventini bacca nutrita Sabina?
Quid quod adulandi gens prudentissima, laudat
Sermonem indocti, faciem deformis amici;
Et longum invalidi collum cervicibus aequat
Herculis, Antaeum procul a tellure tenentis?
Miratur vocem angustam, qua deterius nec   90
Ille sonat, quo mordetur gallina marito.
Haec eadem licet & nobis laudare: sed illis
Creditur. An melior cum Thaida sustinet, aut cum
Uxorem comoedus agit, vel Dorida nullo
Cultam palliolo? Mulier nempe ipsa videtur,
Non persona loqui: vacua & plena omnia dicas
Infra ventriculum & tenui distantia rima.
Nec tamen Antiochus, nec erit mirabilis illic
Aut Stratocles, aut cum molli Demetrius Haemo.
Natio comoeda est. Rides? Majore cachinno   100
Concutitur: flet, si lacrymas aspexit amici:
Nec dolet. Igniculum brumae si tempore poscas,
Accipit endromidem: si dixeris, aestuo, sudat.
Non sumus ergo pares: melior qui semper & omni
Nocte dieque potest alienum sumere vultum;
A facie jactare manus, laudare paratus,
Si bene ructavit, si rectum minxit amicus,
Si trulla inverso crepitum dedit aurea fundo.
Praeterea sanctum nihil est & ab inguine tutum,
Non matrona laris, non filia virgo neque ipse   110
Sponsus laevis adhuc, non filius ante pudicus.
Horum si nihil est, aulam resupinat amici.

sult, to be feared. And since I have started to speak of the Greeks, pass over the gymnasium and hear about a bigger wig's crime: a Stoic was responsible for Barea's death [Barea Soranus, a courageous opponent of Nero]; he informed on his friend, though he himself was a man of mature years and the other was his pupil. He was born on that bank where a feather from the Gorgon's nag [Pegasus] fell to earth [i.e. in Tarsus on the Cydnus]. There is no room for any Roman here: (120) some Protogenes or Diphilus or Erimanthus is lord and master. A national characteristic is the fact that a Greek never shares a patron with anybody else; he keeps him to himself. When he has let fall into his ear a tiny drop of his own and his country's poison, I am driven away from the door; in an instant my long years of servitude have gone for nothing. Nowhere does the loss of a client matter less.

Furthermore (not to flatter ourselves) what use is a poor man's attention and service if, when he goes to the trouble of putting on his toga and hurrying along before daylight, a Praetor urges on his lictor [his official attendant] and orders him to rush at breakneck speed to prevent his colleague from forestalling him in paying his respects to Albina or Modia – childless old ladies who have long been awake? (131) Here the son of freeborn parents gives the inside position to a rich man's slave; for he pays as much as tribunes of a legion earn to Calvina or Catiena in order to shudder on top of her once or twice, whereas you, when you fancy the looks of a dressed-up tart, are in two minds, and hesitate to help Chione down from her high seat. Produce a witness in Rome as honourable as the host of the goddess of Ida [Scipio Nasica], let Numa himself come forward, or the man who rescued the frightened Minerva from the burning shrine [Caecilius Metellus], the first consideration is his money, (140) the last question is about his character. 'How many slaves does he maintain, how many acres of land does he own, how many and how large are his dinner dishes?' Whatever amount of cash a man keeps in his money-box, that is the extent of his reliability. You may swear by the altars of the Samothracian gods and of ours, it is assumed that the poor man treats thunderbolts and gods with contempt and that the gods don't mind. What of the fact that he also provides a motive and material for jokes, if his cloak is filthy and torn, if his toga is grubby, and one shoe gapes open where the leather is split, (150) or if more than one scar is visible where a wound [in his sandal] has

Scire volunt secreta domus atque inde timeri.
Et quoniam coepit Graecorum mentio, transi
Gymnasia atque audi facinus maioris abollae.
Stoicus occidit Baream, delator amicum,
Discipulumque senex, ripa nutritus in illa
Ad quam Gorgonei delapsa est penna caballi.
Non est Romano cuiquam locus hic, ubi regnat
Protogenes aliquis, vel Diphilus, aut Erimanthus,   120
Qui gentis vitio nunquam partitur amicum;
Solus habet. Nam cum facilem stillavit in aurem
Exiguum de naturae patriaeque veneno,
Limine summoveor: perierunt tempora longi
Servitii: nusquam minor est jactura clientis.

   Quod porro officium (ne nobis blandiar) aut quod
Pauperis hic meritum; si curet nocte togatus,
Currere cum Praetor lictorem impellat & ire
Praecipitem jubeat dudum vigilantibus orbis;
Ne prior Albinam aut Modiam collega salutet?   130
Divitis hic servi claudit latus ingenuorum
Filius; alter enim quantum in legione tribuni
Accipiant, donat Calvinae vel Catienae,
Ut semel atque iterum super illam palpitet: at tu
Cum tibi vestiti facies scorti placet, haeres
Et dubitas alta Chionem deducere sella.
Da testem Romae tam sanctum quam fuit hospes
Numinis Idaei: procedat vel Numa vel qui
Servavit trepidam flagranti ex aede Minervam:
Protinus ad censum; de moribus ultima fiet   140
Quaestio: quot pascit servos, quot possidet agri
Jugera, quam multa magnaque paropside coenat.
Quantum quisque sua nummorum servat in arca,
Tantum habet & fidei: jures licet & Samothracum
Et nostrorum aras, contemnere fulmina pauper
Creditur atque deos, diis ignoscentibus ipsis.
Quid quod materiam praebet causasque jocorum
Omnibus hic idem, si foeda & scissa lacerna,
Si toga sordidula est, & rupta calceus alter
Pelle patet; vel si consuto vulnere crassum   150
Atque recens linum ostendit non una cicatrix?

been sewn together with coarse new thread? Of all that unfortunate poverty involves there is nothing more cruel than this: it makes people ridiculous. 'Anyone whose means do not meet the law's demands,' he says [for Otho's law see below] 'will kindly get up and leave the knights' cushioned seats; their places will be taken by the sons of whoremongers born in any brothel; let a sleek auctioneer's boy sit here cheering with the neat young men whose fathers are gladiators or trainers.' That was the wish of the empty-headed Otho, who gave us different seats. [Otho's theatre law gave fourteen rows to the knights, whose fortune was at least 400,000 sesterces. The space immediately in front of the stage was reserved for senators.] (160) Who ever won acceptance here as a son-in-law if he was short of money and failed to match the girl's dowry? What poor man is put down as an heir? Or when is he consulted by the Aediles? The *un*substantial citizens should have long since banded together and walked out. It is no easy thing to rise in the world for those whose abilities are held back by the cramping poverty of their homes; but in Rome their task is especially hard. Wretched accommodation is expensive, servants' bellies are expensive, a meagre supper is expensive. It's a disgrace to eat off earthenware – a practice which you would not regard as shameful if you were suddenly whisked away to the Marsi or to a Samnite table. (170) You'd be satisfied there with a coarse blue hood. In most parts of Italy, to tell the truth, no one puts on a toga except when he's dead. Even when the grand occasion of a public holiday is celebrated in an overgrown theatre and the familiar farce at long last returns to the stage, when the peasant child sitting on his mother's lap is frightened by the gaping white [actor's] mask, even then you'll see the same kind of clothes, with townsfolk and dignitaries dressed alike; the highest officials are content with white tunics as robes for their lofty office. (180) Here in Rome the style of clothes is beyond people's means. Sometimes more than what's needed is borrowed from someone else's money-box. This is a universal fault: here we all live in a state of pretentious poverty. Why go on? Everything in Rome costs money. What do you have to part with to pay your respects once in a while to Cossus, or to win a tight-lipped glance from Veiento [arrogant nobles]? One is attending the first shave, another the first haircut of a favourite boy; the house is full of cakes for sale. 'Take the money and keep your bit of yeast!' We clients have to pay contributions to smartly dressed slaves and add to their savings. [The client is expected to buy the cake from the slave and then offer it to the patron's household gods.]

Nil habet infelix paupertas durius in se
Quam quod ridiculos homines facit: Exeat, inquit,
Si pudor est, & de pulvino surgat equestri,
Cujus res legi non sufficit, & sedeant hic
Lenonum pueri quocunque in fornice nati.
Hic plaudat nitidi praeconis filius inter
Pinnirapi cultos juvenes, juvenesque lanistae.
Sic libitum vano, qui nos distinxit, Othoni.
Quis gener hic placuit censu minor atque puellae   160
Sarcinulis impar? quis pauper scribitur haeres?
Quando in consilio est aedilibus? agmine facto
Debuerant olim tenues migrasse Quirites.
Haud facile emergunt, quorum virtutibus obstat
Res angusta domi. Sed Romae durior illis
Conatus: magno hospitium miserabile, magno
Servorum ventres, & frugi coenula magno.
Fictilibus coenare pudet, quod turpe negabis
Translatus subito ad Marsos mensamque Sabellam,
Contentusque illic Veneto duroque cucullo.   170
Pars magna Italiae est (si verum admittimus) in qua
Nemo togam sumit nisi mortuus. Ipsa dierum
Festorum herboso colitur si quando theatro
Majestas: tandemque redit ad pulpita notum
Exodium, cum personae pallentis hiatum
In gremio matris formidat rusticus infans;
Aequales habitus illic, similemque videbis
Orchestram & populum; clari velamen honoris,
Sufficiunt tunicae summis Aedilibus albae.
Hic ultra vires habitus nitor: hic aliquid plus   180
Quam satis est interdum aliena sumitur arca.
Commune id vitium est: hic vivimus ambitiosa
Paupertate omnes: quid te moror? Omnia Romae
Cum pretio. Quid das ut Cossum aliquando salutes?
Ut te respiciat clauso Veiento labello?
Ille metit barbam, crinem hic deponit amati:
Plena domus libis venalibus: accipe & illud
Fermentum tibi habe: praestare tributa clientes
Cogimur & cultis augere peculia servis.

(190) Who is afraid or has ever been afraid of his house falling down in cool Praeneste, or in Volsinii among its tree-clad hills, or in simple Gabii, or in the fastness of Tibur above its steep slope? We live in a city which, for the most part, is held up by rickety props – that's how the landlord's agent prevents collapse. He patches up a yawning gap in the old wall and then assures you you can sleep at ease, when the structure is on the point of caving in. One should live in a place where there are no fires, no nightly scares. Already Ucalegon is shouting 'Fire!' and moving his bits and pieces. Now the third floor of *your* building is smoking, (200) but you know nothing about it. If the alarm is raised at the bottom of the staircase, the last man to fry will be the one who is protected from the rain only by the tiles where the gentle doves lay their eggs. Codrus had a bed which would have been too small for Procula [presumably a dwarf], six little water pots to adorn his sideboard, also a small mug underneath and a Chiron [a centaur] couchant below the same slab of marble. A now ancient chest contained some Greek books, and the inspired poems were being gnawed by illiterate mice. Codrus had nothing – all right, but the poor fellow lost that nothing, every bit of it. (209) And what puts the cap on his misery is the fact that when he hasn't a stitch and is begging for scraps no one will help him with food or lodging or shelter. But if Asturius' great house is destroyed, the nobles appear in black and their ladies with dishevelled hair; the Praetor adjourns his court. Then we lament the disasters of the city; then we curse fire. Before the flames have gone out, one man rushes up to offer marble or a gift of building materials, another provides shining nude statues; this man presents some splendid work of Euphranor or Polyclitus [Greek sculptors] – ancient ornaments of Phaecasian divinities; another gives books and cases and a figure of Minerva to stand in the middle; another a bagful of money. (220) Persicus, the richest of all childless men, replaces his losses with more numerous and more expensive items, and he is now with reason suspected of having set fire to his own house. If you can tear yourself away from the races, a first-rate house can be bought outright at Sora or Fabrateria or Frusino for the price you now pay to rent a dark hole for a year. There you will have a plot and a shallow well from which water can easily be drawn without a rope and poured over all your delicate plants. If you live wedded to your hoe and look after your well-tended garden you'll be able to provide a feast for a hundred Pythagoreans [vegetarian philosophers]. (230) It is something in any place, however remote, to become the owner of a single lizard.

Quis timet aut timuit gelida Praeneste ruinam,   190
Aut positis nemorosa inter juga Volsiniis, aut
Simplicibus Gabiis, aut proni Tiburis arce?
Nos urbem colimus tenui tibicine fultam
Magna parte sui: nam sic labentibus obstat
Villicus & veteris rimae cum texit hiatum,
Securos pendente jubet dormire ruina.
Vivendum est illic ubi nulla incendia, nulli
Nocte metus: jam poscit aquam, jam frivola transfert
Ucalegon; tabulata tibi jam tertia fumant.
Tu nescis. Nam si gradibus trepidatur ab imis,   200
Ultimus ardebit quem tegula sola tuetur
A pluvia, molles ubi reddunt ova columbae.
Lectus erat Codro Procula minor, urceoli sex,
Ornamentum abaci; necnon & parvulus infra
Cantharus & recubans sub eodem marmore Chiron;
Jamque vetus Graecos servabat cista libellos,
Et divina opici rodebant carmina mures.
Nil habuit Codrus: quis enim negat? Et tamen illud
Perdidit infelix totum nil: ultimus autem
Aerumnae cumulus, quod nudum & frusta rogantem   210
Nemo cibo, nemo hospitio, tectoque juvabit.
Si magna Asturii cecidit domus, horrida mater,
Pullati proceres, differt vadimonia praetor:
Tunc gemimus casus urbis, tunc odimus ignem.
Ardet adhuc & jam accurrit qui marmora donet,
Conferat impensas. Hic nuda & candida signa;
Hic aliquid praeclarum Euphranoris & Polycleti,
Phaecasianorum vetera ornamenta deorum.
Hic libros dabit & forulos mediamque Minervam;
Hic modium argenti: meliora ac plura reponit   220
Persicus orborum lautissimus & merito jam
Suspectus, tanquam ipse suas incenderit aedes.
Si potes avelli Circensibus, optima Sorae
Aut Fabrateriae domus aut Frusinone paratur,
Quanti nunc tenebras unum conducis in annum.
Hortulus hic, puteusque brevis, nec reste movendus,
In tenues plantas facili diffunditur haustu.
Vive bidentis amans & culti villicus horti,
Unde epulum possis centum dare Pythagoraeis.
Est aliquid quocunque loco, quocunque recessu,   230
Unius sese dominum fecisse lacertae.

Here most invalids die from lack of sleep, the illness being caused by undigested food lying on a feverish stomach. For when is sleep possible in rented rooms? It costs a lot of money to sleep in the city. That's the root of the complaint. The coming and going of vehicles in the narrow twisty streets and the abuse of a herd which has been brought to a standstill banish sleep even from Drusus or a seal. If duty calls, the crowd will fall back and (240) the rich man will be carried along, speeding above the upturned faces in a huge Liburnian galley [a litter described as if it were a naval vessel], while he is installed inside, reading, writing, or taking a nap on the way, for the litter with its closed windows is conducive to sleep. Yet he'll still get there before us. As we hurry along, a wave stands in the way and the crowd pressing behind us in a huge mass crushes the base of our spines. One fellow hits you with his elbow, another with a hard litter-pole; one strikes your head with a beam, another with a wine jar. My legs are caked with mud; a minute later I am trampled with big feet from every side, and a soldier stamps on my toes with his hob-nailed sandal. Look at all the smoke there; a crowd is holding a picnic. (250) There are a hundred guests, each with a portable kitchen carried behind him. Corbulo himself [a famous general] could hardly lift so many huge utensils and pile so many things on his head as the poor little slave carries along with head erect, fanning the flame as he runs. Mended tunics are ripped; now a tall fir sways on a waggon as it approaches; a pine is carried on another. Both trees wave menacingly over the people from above. If the axle carrying Ligurian marble gives way and tips its mountainous load over on top of the crowd, what is left of their bodies? Who can discover their limbs or bones? (260) The body of the man in the street is completely crushed out of existence, just like his soul. Meantime the folks at home, happily unaware of what has happened, are now washing the dishes, blowing the fire to a flame, clattering the oily scrapers, filling the jug, and laying out the towels. The house-boys are busy at their various jobs, but he is already sitting on the bank, a new arrival, trembling in fear of the sinister ferryman [Charon]; the poor fellow has no hope of a place on the boat which plies on the muddy waters, having no coin to hold out between his lips.

Plurimus hic aeger moritur vigilando; sed illum
Languorem peperit cibus imperfectus & haerens
Ardenti stomacho. Nam quae meritoria somnum
Admittunt? Magnis opibus dormitur in urbe.
Inde caput morbi: rhedarum transitus arcto
Vicorum in flexu & stantis convicia mandrae
Eripient somnum Druso vitulisque marinis.
Si vocat officium turba cedente vehetur
Dives & ingenti curret super ora Liburno,   240
Atque obiter leget aut scribet vel dormiet intus.
Namque facit somnum clausa lectica fenestra.
Ante tamen veniet: nobis properantibus obstat
Unda prior, magno populus premit agmine lumbos
Qui sequitur: ferit hic cubito, ferit assere duro
Alter; at hic tignum capiti incutit, ille metretam;
Pinguia crura luto; planta mox undique magna
Calcor & in digito clavus mihi militis haeret.
Nonne vides quanto celebretur sportula fumo?
Centum convivae; sequitur sua quemque culina.   250
Corbulo vix ferret tot vasa ingentia, tot res
Impositas capiti, quas recto vertice portat
Servulus infelix & cursu ventilat ignem.
Scinduntur tunicae sartae; modo longa coruscat
Sarraco veniente abies, atque altera pinum
Plaustra vehunt, nutant alte populoque minantur.
Nam si procubuit, qui saxa Ligustica portat
Axis, & eversum fudit super agmina montem,
Quid superest de corporibus? Quis membra, quis ossa
Invenit? Obtritum vulgi perit omne cadaver,   260
More animae. Domus interea secura patellas
Jam lavat & bucca foculum excitat & sonat unctis
Striglibus & pleno componit lintea gutto.
Haec inter pueros varie properantur: at ille
Jam sedet in ripa, tetrumque novitius horret
Porthmea, nec sperat coenosi gurgitis alnum
Infelix, nec habet quem porrigat ore trientem.

Consider now various other nocturnal dangers – how far it is up to that high roof from which a sherd smashes your brains, (270) as often as leaky and broken bits of crockery fall from the windows, and with what an impact they strike the pavement, leaving it chipped and shattered. You could well be thought negligent and ill-prepared for sudden accident if you went out to dinner without making your will. There is a separate form of death that night in every window which watches you with open shutters as you pass underneath. So you should hope and pray with piteous sincerity that they may be content to throw down just the contents of their wide basins.

The drunken thug, who for some reason has failed to kill anyone, pays the price; he goes through a night of agony, as the son of Peleus [Achilles] did when he mourned his friend [Patroclus], lying one moment on his face another on his back. (281) So he will be unable to get to sleep in any other way; some people can only sleep after a brawl. But although he is at a wild age and his blood is heated with wine, he carefully leaves alone the man whose safe passage is guaranteed by his scarlet cloak, his endless line of attendants, and the flames from his numerous bronze lamps. But he treats *me* with contempt; for I am usually escorted home by the moon or the faint light of a lamp whose wick I tend and eke out. This is how a miserable fight begins – if you can call it a fight when someone else delivers the punches and I just take them. (290) He stands in my way and orders me to halt. One has to obey; what else is there to do when one is at the mercy of a madman who is also stronger than oneself? 'Where have you been?' he roars. 'Whose rot-gut and beans have given you wind? With what cobbler have you been scoffing leek-tips and a boiled sheep's head? You won't answer? Talk or else here's a kick. Tell me, where's your beggar's stand? In what synagogue can I find you?' It's all the same whether you try to say something or to slip quietly away; they still beat you up, and then, outraged, take you to court. This is the poor man's freedom: (300) after being severely punched and beaten he asks and begs permission to go home with a few teeth left.

Nor is this all you have to fear. When your house is shut, when your shop is all secured by chains and every shutter is locked and silent, there will always be someone to rob you. Sometimes a murderer does his job quickly with a knife. When the Pontine Marshes and the Gallinarian pine-forest are made safe by armed patrols, then they all converge eagerly on Rome as if it were a game reserve.

    Respice nunc alia ac diversa pericula noctis:
Quod spatium tectis sublimibus, unde cerebrum
Testa ferit, quoties rimosa & curta fenestris   270
Vasa cadunt, quanto percussum pondere signent
Et laedant silicem. Possis ignavus haberi
Et subiti casus improvidus, ad coenam si
Intestatus eas, adeo tot fata, quot illa
Nocte patent vigiles, te praetereunte, fenestrae.
Ergo optes, votumque feras miserabile tecum,
Ut sint contentae patulas effundere pelves.
Ebrius ac petulans, qui nullum forte cecidit,
Dat poenas, noctem patitur lugentis amicum
Pelidae, cubat in faciem, mox deinde supinus.   280
Ergo non aliter poterit dormire: quibusdam
Somnum rixa facit: sed quamvis improbus annis
Atque mero fervens, cavet hunc quem coccina laena
Vitari jubet & comitum longissimus ordo,
Multum praeterea flammarum atque aenea lampas.
Me, quem Luna solet deducere vel breve lumen
Candelae, cujus dispenso & tempero filum,
Contemnit. Miserae cognosce prooemia rixae,
Si rixa est, ubi tu pulsas, ego vapulo tantum.
Stat contra starique jubet; parere necesse est.   290
Nam quid agas, cum te furiosus cogat & idem
Fortior? Unde venis? Exclamat: cujus aceto,
Cujus conche tumes? Quis tecum sectile porrum
Sutor & elixi vervecis labra comedit?
Nil mihi respondes? Aut dic aut accipe calcem.
Ede ubi consistas: in qua te quaero proseucha?
Dicere si tentes aliquid, tacitusque recedas,
Tantundem est: feriunt pariter: vadimonia deinde
Irati faciunt. Libertas pauperis haec est:
Pulsatus rogat & pugnis concisus adorat   300
Ut liceat paucis cum dentibus inde reverti.
Nec tamen hoc tantum metuas. Nam qui spoliet te
Non deerit, clausis domibus, postquam omnis ubique
Fixa catenatae siluit compago tabernae.
Interdum & ferro subitus grassator agit rem:
Armato quoties tutae custode tenentur
Et Pomptina palus & Gallinaria pinus,
Sic inde huc omnes tanquam ad vivaria currunt.

What forge, what anvil is without heavy chains? (310) The chief use of iron is for fetters; in fact one fears a shortage of ploughshares and the disappearance of hoes and mattocks. Happy, one feels, were our great grandfathers' ancestors, happy was the period which, under the kings and tribunes of old, saw Rome content with a single jail.

I could add many other reasons to these; but the mules are calling me, the sun's going down, and it's time to be off. The driver has been signalling to me for some time by waving his whip. So goodbye, and don't forget me. Whenever Rome allows you a quick trip to your native Aquinum for the sake of your health, tear me away from Cumae to the shrines which Helvius built for Ceres and your people built for Diana. I shall put on my heavy boots and come to your chilly part of the country to help your satires, if they're not ashamed to have me.

Qua fornace graves, qua non incude catenae?
Maximus in vinclis ferri modus, ut timeas ne   310
Vomer deficiat, ne marrae & sarcula desint.
Felices proavorum atavos, felicia dicas
Saecula quae quondam sub regibus atque tribunis
Viderunt uno contentam carcere Romam.

His alias poteram & plures subnectere causas:
Sed jumenta vocant & sol inclinat; eundum est.
Nam mihi commota jamdudum mulio virga
Innuit: ergo vale nostri memor; et quoties te
Roma tuo refici properantem reddet Aquino,
Me quoque ad Elvinam Cererem vestramque Dianam
Convelle a Cumis; satirarum ego (ni pudet illas)
Adjutor gelidos veniam caligatus in agros.

NOTE
Except for a few minor changes, the text printed above is that of the Delphin
edition by L. Prateus (1684). A small number of bowdlerized passages have been
supplied from a later printing of the same edition. The Delphin differs from the
Oxford Classical Text at several points, of which the most important are as follows (the Delphin reading is given first):

18f.   *praestantius* and *aquae* genitive: *praesentius* and *aquae* dative
36f.   *vulgi Quemlibet: uulgus cum iubet*
61   *Achaeae: Achaei*
77   *Magus: omnia novit.: magus, omnia nouit*
        (In the text accompanying *London* Johnson read *Magus: omnia novit*)
105f.   *alienum sumere vultum,: aliena sumere uultum*
112   *aulam: auiam* (see note)
113   printed: excluded as a gloss
168   *negavit: negabis* (*negavit* cannot be right)
218   *Phaecasianorum: haec Asianorum* (*Phaecasianus* was supposed to mean
        'wearing white shoes')
238   *eripiunt: eripient*
254   *sartae: modo: sartae modo,* (recently mended)
218   printed: excluded as a gloss
        (At 320 the Latin text which accompanied *London* had the unmetrical
        reading *Me quoque ad Eleusinam Cererem* etc. The adjective 'Eleusinian'
        referred to the worship of Ceres at Eleusis. Bloom and Bloom (1) 22
        believe that by combining this text with 'the wilds of Kent' Johnson
        meant the reader to think of Canterbury Cathedral. See note on
        London 257.)
321   *Convelle: conuerte*
322   *Adjutor: auditor*

NOTES ON *LONDON*

Epigraph: 'Who is so willing to put up with the foolish city, who so iron of soul as to contain himself?' – a quotation from Juv. 1.30-31; but Juvenal wrote, not *ineptae* (foolish), but *iniquae* (unjust or wicked) – a much stronger word. Probably just a slip on J's part.

2 Thales: traditionally understood as Thales of Miletus (early 6th cent. B.C.), a pioneer of Greek natural philosophy. If this is right, the name typifies 'the wise man'; and that is all J's reader was expected to know. The further suggestion, in Bloom (1), that J took the name specifically from Juv. 13.184-5, where Thales is spoken of as 'a gentle soul' (*mite ingenium*), is only a remote possibility; for there Thales exemplifies the philosopher who calmly accepts crime and injustice. A more recent proposal, in Bate (2) 172, is that Thales recalls the Greek lyric poet of the 7th cent. B.C. whom Lycurgus is said to have brought from Crete to Sparta (Plutarch, *Lycurgus* 4). His odes induced such harmony and obedience that he was thought of as a kind of lawgiver. On this view J.'s Thales has been rejected by the community which he sought to civilize. This is more plausible, for (unlike Juv.'s Umbricius) J.'s Thales is a poet (260ff.), though not a *lyric* poet, and Plutarch's *Lives* were familiar to J.'s readers. But certainty is impossible.

Another question is whether J.'s picture of Thales was influenced by the case of his friend, the poet Richard Savage, who left London to live in Swansea in July 1739. This was after the publication of *London*, but Savage's departure may have been proposed long enough before to have entered J.'s mind. Retrospectively, at least, he seems to have associated the two figures; for in the Dict. under sense 2 of 'dissipate' he quoted a sentence from his *Life of Savage* and then under sense 3 quoted v.20 of *London*. All this, however, does not justify the crude equation of Thales with Savage – an equation which J. himself denied and which, even after 1739, would have been quite unnecessary for an understanding of the poem. See on 69-70 and 81 below.

3-4 Oldham had
> Though much concern'd to leave my dear old Friend,
> I must however his Design commend

(*Poems and Translations*. By the Author of *The Satyrs upon the Jesuits*, London 1683, 180.)

4 The compressed antithesis combines two ideas: 'I praise his decision to become a hermit' and 'I regret the loss of my friend'.
Hermit: here not literally an anchorite, but one who leads a solitary life; cf. 'cell' (49).

5 Who now resolves: strictly speaking Thales had already made his decision. The reading 'Resolved at length' (1787) removes this negligible blemish but involves a less straightforward syntax, for 'Resolved' must be in the accusative (or objective) case agreeing with 'friend' rather than in the nominative with 'I'.

7-8 Fix'd: not 'determined', but 'settled'; cf. Juv.'s *sedem figere* (2).·In his *Polyolbion* 5.333-43 (a poem which J admired) Drayton had referred to 'holy David's seat' in 'Cambria'.

True Briton: Thales' withdrawal is a sign of his patriotism. Juv.'s Umbricius leaves 'the Greek metropolis' for Cumae, a Greek colony. If irony was intended by Juv. the point is not obvious.

9-10 Hibernia's land: Ireland. The periphrasis carries the idea of 'wintry' (Lat. *hibernus*), which balances 'the rocks of Scotland'.

Strand: there is a play on 'strand' (as opposed to 'rocks') and 'Strand' (the London street). J. has expanded the geography of Oldham:

> The Peake, the Fens, the Hundreds, or Lands-end,
> I would prefer to Fleetstreet, or the Strand. (181)

When J. first arrived in London, he had lodgings off the Strand 'in an upper room of a house in Exeter St., behind Exeter 'change, inhabited by one Norris a stay-maker', Hawkins, *Life of Johnson*, 57. Boswell was wrong to regard J.'s lines as an example of anti-Scottish prejudice; for the sense is 'Ireland and Scotland are grim, but London is a lot worse'.

13-17 T. S. Eliot criticized these lines as lacking in authenticity. See 'Johnson as Critic and Poet' in *On Poetry and Poets*, London 1957. No doubt there is some overstatement (though less than in Juv.), but the features mentioned can all be abundantly documented. In 1738 many areas of London, especially the older districts, were still highly dangerous. See George 81-4, Plumb 13-22, Weinbrot 166-9.

16 Fell: cruel and inhuman.

Attorney: an officer of the Common Law Court. As attorneys were often over-zealous in applying the harsh Settlement and Vagrancy laws, they were hated by the poor. Fielding called them 'pests of society'. See Turberville i, 309-11. J.'s 'attorney' may have been prompted by Boileau's *le Sergent*:

> Allons du moins chercher quelque antre ou quelque roche,
> D'ou jamais ni l'Huissier, ni le Sergent n'approche.
> (*Sat.* 1.25-6)

17 Falling houses: 'Two things are conspicuous in the London of the eighteenth century. One, the number of old ruinous houses which frequently collapsed', George 73; see also 74-5.

18 In its bathos this is designed as a parallel to Juv.'s 'poets reciting in the month of August'. The idea of killing may owe something to *paene enecabant* in Schrevelius' note, but it is better to recall Pope, *Essay on Critism* (624):

> Nay, fly to Altars; there they'll talk you dead.

19 Wherry: a light river-boat which will take Thales out to his ship. See 255.

20 Dissipated: Thales has been unable to bear the exorbitant cost of living in London. There can hardly be any hint of condemnation here, for Thales is a virtuous man. For the sense cf. 'spent' in 256.

21-4 J. had lodgings in Greenwich for a short period in the summer of 1737. *London*, however, was written at no. 6, Castle St., near Cavendish Square, not at Greenwich.

22 One might have expected a contrast, as in Juv., between squalid present and more attractive past, but the contrast in J. is a *political* contrast. The scene at Greenwich is *not* squalid, and it is a mistake to find overtones of commercial greed in 'the silver flood'.

23 Struck: strongly impressed.

Eliza: Queen Elizabeth was born at Greenwich. Nostalgia for the Elizabethan age was widespread among Walpole's critics, especially in the circle of Bolingbroke; see Kramnick's index under *Elizabeth*.

27 Cross: the cross of St. George.

Main: the high seas. For the sentiments compare Arne's 'Rule Britannia', which was heard for the first time in the musical drama *The Masque of Alfred* (1740).

29 Masquerades: masked balls.

Excise: by the bonded warehouse system imported goods were kept in a warehouse until sold to retailers, when a duty was paid. This was applied to tea, coffee, and a few other commodities in 1723; ten years later Walpole proposed to extend the scheme to cover wine and tobacco, hoping to use the revenue to abolish the land tax. But the opposition played on people's fear of government interference, and the idea was eventually dropped.

30 See on 53-4 below.

33-4 Dryden had:
> Then thus Umbritius, with angry frown
> And looking back on this degen'rate town.   (37-8)

This does not correspond to anything in Juv., but the speaker's anger had already been made explicit by Boileau (*Sat.* 1.19-20) and Oldham (181).

36 In Juv. 1.74 worth is praised – and shivers (*probitas laudatur et alget*); in J. it lacks even this amount of tribute.

37 Devote: devoted.

38 Science: men engaged in intellectual work.

Unrewarded...in vain: an intentional pleonasm used for emphasis.

39 But sooths: soothes but.

40-42 Note the alliteration, which is not merely a decorative device but enforces the sense.

40 Moment: the subject of 'leaves'.

42 Revels: not 'delights', but 'runs riotously'.

45 Osiers: willows.

47 Harrass'd Briton: a reference to the Anglo-Saxon invasions of the 5th and 6th centuries. The new invasion turns out to be French.

49 Cell: the word, which can mean any small dwelling, does not imply that Thales is actually going to become a solitary monk; but like 'hermit' (4) it has religious overtones.

50 The monosyllabic name was never supplied. X has adapted to London as a worm adapts
to dirt. J. may have had in mind
> Que George vive ici, puisque George y sait vivre
> > (Boileau, *Sat.* 1.34)

in which case the shaft is aimed at George II.

51 Pensions: J. was indignant at the allowances dispensed by Walpole, but many years
later (1762) he accepted a pension himself.

52 Patriot: at this time the name belonged to a heterogeneous group of Whigs and Tories,
led by Pulteney and Bolingbroke. (For a fuller list see Grant Robertson, 53.) These
men, who included some very able writers, attacked Walpole in plays, pamphlets,
ballads, and especially in *The Craftsman*. They found an ally in the Prince of Wales,
who was on bad terms with the king and had set up a separate court at Leicester
House in 1736.

53-4 Dear-bought rights: Probably J. means commercial rights. Since 1713 England was
entitled to supply Spanish colonies with negro slaves and to send one ship a year to
trade at Cartagena or Vera Cruz. When these rights were illegally extended by
British merchants the Spaniards retaliated by conducting searches in mid ocean,
often with considerable violence. This and other causes led to a crisis. Walpole, who
was anxious to settle the differences by negotiation, was vilified as an appeaser. J.
himself notes sarcastically 'The invasions of the Spaniards were defended in the
houses of Parliament'. Newcastle, Pitt, and the rest of the opposition were bent on
war, which finally came in 1739 (the War of Jenkins' Ear). See Williams 207-10,
Grant Robertson 77-80 and Appendix 3.
In the face of day: in broad daylight.

55 'It is impossible to taint a body already poisoned.' This objection was made by William
Mudford in 1802 and by William Shaw before him. In fact J. has used a Latin con-
struction whereby the adjective 'poison'd' is proleptic – i.e. taken before its time.
The sense is 'taint our youth so that it becomes poisoned'.

58 Farm a lottery: 'Even the Government exploited the universal craze for gambling by
raising state lotteries, which were patronized by all classes in society' (Turberville i,
355).

59 Warbling eunuchs: the *castrati* of Italian opera, which was then in fashion.
A licens'd stage: Walpole's Licensing Act (1737) was a response to repeated attacks
on the government over the previous decade by Gay, Fielding, and others. It limited
the number of theatres, and required that all plays and operas should be submitted
to the Lord Chamberlain at least a fortnight before they were due to open. See P. J.
Crean, 'The Stage Licensing Act of 1737', *Modern Philology* 35 (1937-8) 239-55.
The original reading was 'our silenc'd stage', which involved a contradiction after
'warbling'. In any case, by 1748, with Walpole dead and Garrick manager at Drury
Lane, the idea of 'silenc'd' was inappropriate. Yet the reading was restored in 1787.

60 Thoughtless: too stupid to care.

61 Pride: objective case.

65 A groaning nation's spoils: spoils taken from a groaning nation. The 1st ed., and that
of 1787, had 'the plunder of a land is given' – a lighter and less tightly packed expression.

66 Public crimes: crimes against the people.

69-70 'I can hardly refrain from showing up a poet as second-rate and derivative, even though he has a title and writes in praise of the court.' In Horace, *Epist.* 1.3.18-20 Celsus is advised to rely more on his own resources – otherwise the birds may come to reclaim their plumage and the poor crow will become an object of ridicule. This is an adaptation of the Aesopic fable found in Babrius 72 and Phaedrus 1.3. J. may well be referring to Cibber, who became poet laureate in 1730; cf. the ironical passage in J.'s *Compleat Vindication of the Licensers of the Stage* (1739), where the writer imagines 'those Halcyon-days in which no politicks shall be read but those of the Gazetteer [cf. v.72] nor any poetry but that of the Laureat'. This, however, does not prove the equation Thales = Savage, even though the latter resented Cibber's appointment and set himself up as 'Volunteer Laureate'. All it means is that Thales shares Savage's (and others') dislike of Cibber and is sorely tempted to expose his inadequacies.

72 Gazetteer: *The Daily Gazetteer*, founded in 1735, was the official newspaper of Walpole's government.

73 One who spends half his allowance on clothes.

74 H——y's: traditionally identified as John, Lord Hervey (1696-1743), Walpole's supporter and confidant of the queen, known to Pope's readers as 'Sporus' and 'Lord Fanny'. But Greene (307-8) argues strongly for John, 'Orator' Henley (1692-1756). Preacher, exhibitionist and wit, Henley was employed by Walpole in 1730 to ridicule *The Craftsman* in a periodical called *The Hyp Doctor*. For a full study see G. Midgeley, *The Life of Orator Henley*, Oxford 1973.

'Clodio's' was substituted in the 1787 edition, by which time Hervey and Henley were both long dead. As 'Clodio' was derived from the Lat. *claudus* (lame) it suited a feeble wit, and it was in line with other 'significant' names like 'Orgilio' and 'Balbo'. It is not clear, however, that Hawkins had J.'s authority for the change.

79 Rustick: used here, not without irony, to suggest the simple, wholesome country as opposed to the false, over-sophisticated city. Cf. Boileau: *Je suis rustique et fier, et j'ai l'ame grossiere* (*Sat.* 1.50).

80 Puzzle: to complicate and so obscure.

81 Spy: Savage was accused of spying for Pope (*Lives of the Poets* ii, 362, ed. Hill); but where there are factions there are always informers (cf. 252 below), and so here, too, it is best to see Thales as a figure who shares certain views and experiences with Savage.

83 Here, for variety, the antithesis is presented in chiastic order – ABBA.

83-4 Friendship of this kind is based on complicity and the mutual fear of exposure. 'Social', from Lat. *socialis*, means 'pertaining to companionship', hence 'shared'; but the phrase 'social guilt' looks like an original stroke of wit.

Orgilio: a name implying arrogance (Italian *orgóglio*, French *orgeuil*). The obsolete *'orgillous'* is given in the Dict. See on 208.

86 See Marlborough and Villiers (2) in list.

89 Self-approving: having a good conscience. Smugness is not implied; cf. *se probare* in, e.g., Horace, *Sat.* 1.1.109.

91 The favourites who prosper, thanks to the nation which they cheat. Partly Italians, but mainly French.

92 The antecedent of 'who' is 'the great'.

94 Shore: Oldham had

> the Common-shore
> Where France does all her Filth and Ordure pour (185).

It seems that J. came to regard 'sewer' as the more correct form (see Dict. under 'shore'); in any case 'sewer' was substituted in editions after 1758. The later reading also avoided the ambiguity of 'shore'. Cf. Dryden (110-11):

> Obscene Orontes, diving under ground,
> Conveys his wealth to Tyber's hungry shores.

98 As in more recent times, French elegance was regarded with a mixture of admiration and suspicion. In this respect the French provided a suitable counterpart to Juv.'s Greeks. Greece, however, did not present any military threat to Rome, whereas French power under Cardinal Fleury had been allowed to develop as a result of Walpole's foreign policy. Anti-French feeling was widespread. 'The London populace still continued its traditional hostility to foreigners, who were generally classed indiscriminately as French' (George, 133). Yet the fascination remained. For an illustration of the popularity of French fashions see the passage quoted by J. H. Plumb in *Sir Robert Walpole: the Making of a Statesman*, London 1956, 28-9.

99 Edward: see list.

Realms of day: heaven, earth being a dark vale of sin and woe.

102 Surly grace: here, as in 'surly virtue' (145), 'surly' is best understood as 'rough'.

103 'Lost' agrees with 'warrior' (104). For 'thoughtless' see on 60.

104 The warrior has dwindled to a beau, who (sense, freedom, and piety having been refined away) is the mimic of France etc. 'Refined away' is ironical, since the expression is normally used of impurities. Dryden had

> Your herdsman primitive, your homely clown
> Is turn'd a beau in a loose tawdry gown. (119-20)

108 Gibbet: gallows.

Wheel: a method of execution used in France before the revolution, when it was replaced by the guillotine. The victim was spreadeagled, and then as the wheel revolved his bones were broken with an iron bar. Sometimes the executioner was ordered to finish the prisoner off; the blows were then called *coups de grâce*.

112 Fond: foolishly well disposed.

114 : Clean shoes: cf. Oldham (186):

> Foot-boys at first, till they, from wiping Shooes,
> Grow by degrees the Masters of the House.

Clap: gonorrhoea, 'the French disease'. Note the descending order of accomplishments.

115 Fasting Monsieur: Oldham (186) had 'A needy Monsieur'.

116 Go to hell: by putting *in caelum . . . ibit* (78), 'he will mount to the skies', Juv. had in mind simply a physical absurdity. Dryden (141) wrote 'And bid him go to heav'n, to heav'n he goes', which implied instead a religious injunction. J. saw that this could be improved, for no Englishman ever told anyone to 'go to heaven'.

117-8 Cf. Oldham (187)

> Then, pray, what mighty Privilege is there
> For me, that at my Birth drew English Air?

119 Right: object of 'to prize'. Britons have forfeited their birthright (i.e. liberty) by surrendering to the flattery of the French.

120 Henry's victories: Agincourt (1415) and other victories over the French, leading to the Treaty of Troyes (1420). For Henry see list. J. may have in mind the patriotic recollection of St. Crispin's day as foreseen by the king in Shakespeare's *Henry V* 4.3.51ff., especially v. 56: 'This story shall the good man teach his son.'

121 A satirical version of Horace's famous words

> Graecia capta ferum victorem cepit (*Epist.* 2.1.156)
> Greece, on being captured, took her rough conqueror captive.

122 Early editions read

> And what their armies lost, their cringes gain?

This was a little untidy in that one had to apply 'their' to the French after understanding 'conqueror' of the English. Hence, presumably, the alteration. Later, in 1787, Hawkins (on whose authority?) read 'prevails' instead of 'subdues', perhaps because it gave a more exact balance to 'are vain'.

124 Supple: easily assuming any posture, especially one of deference.
Parasite: 'one that frequents rich tables, and earns his welcome by flattery', Dict.

125-6 'True' agrees with 'tongue'. Some editions, on the false but excusable assumption that it agreed with 'Gaul', put a full stop after 'goes'.

126-8 J. exploits the ambiguity of 'bestow', which can mean 'attribute' or, literally, 'confer'. In 127f. he assumes the second sense, as if people's looks and speech had *actually* been transformed.

129-31 The only triplet in J.'s mature verse (Nichol Smith). Unlike Juv.'s Umbricius (92), Thales does not include himself among the hypocrites.

130 With diffidence: without confidence.

131 Gain: Hawkins (on whose authority?) changed this to 'get', perhaps on account of the sequence 'vain', 'strain', 'gain'. Yet the internal rhymes are defensible in a triplet.

140 J. concentrates Oldham's couplet (188)

> Do you but smile, immediately the Beast
> Laughs out aloud, tho he ne'er heard the jest.

142-3 The indispensable rhyme 'heat'/'sweat' was used by Oldham (188) and Dryden (177-8).
Hints: mentions.

143 Dog-days: the period when the Dogstar Sirius rises and sets with the sun (3 July to 11 August); a time of oppressive heat, at least in Mediterranean countries.

145 Surly: see on 102.
Fix a friend: make a firm friend.

146 Slaves: in apposition to 'competitors' (144).
Serious impudence: shamelessness with a serious expression.

149 The line should be enclosed, at least mentally, in parentheses, for 'taste' exemplifies 'trifle', and 'judgment' exemplifies 'vice'.

150 In his original draft J. had written
Who dwell on Balbo's courtly mien [i.e. looks].
But since Balbo comes from the Lat. *balbus* (stammering), the change to 'eloquence' was clearly an improvement. No individual can be identified.

151 Writing of James I, Sir Anthony Weldon said 'His walk was ever circular, his fingers ever in that walke fidling about his cod-piece', quoted in *James I by his Contemporaries*, ed. Robert Ashton, London 1969, 12.

153 'Invade' has a literal (though extended) sense with 'table', a figurative sense with 'breast'; an instance of zeugma.

155 Reading the absurd *aulam* in Juv. 112, and accepting the probably spurious 113, Barten Holyday translated:
They'll ransack House and Heart and thence be fear'd.
His note explains: 'He will turn his friend's house and all in it, as it were, upside down, so to discover his secrets and keep him in awe.' This was taken over and condensed by J. in 154-5.

157 Commence: 'to take a new character', Dict. Hence 'to turn into' or 'become'.

158 By numbers: on account of their large numbers.

160 Rigid: severe, cf. 16 above.

161 Snarling muse: satire. In classical times the satirist was sometimes referred to as as a vicious cur by his opponents and as a trusty watch-dog by his supporters. See, e.g., Horace, *Epodes* 6, *Sat.* 2.1.85; Diogenes Laertius 6.60.

162 Sober: solemn, with overtones of 'humourless'.

163 Dream: i.e. of riches, cf. 184.
Labours for a joke: struggles to make a joke.

164 Brisker: more lively and alert.

168 Gen'rous: noble.

169 Blockhead's insult: i.e. an insulting blockhead.
Points: 'directs' rather than 'sharpens', for sharpening would imply wit.

170-75 These lines are based on Horace's sixteenth epode, where the poet calls on those who are disgusted with civil war to set forth on 'the encircling ocean' and to seek 'the happy land' and 'the rich islands' which Jupiter has 'reserved' (*secrevit*) for the righteous. The association was prompted by Juv.'s *debuerant migrasse ... Quirites*

(163). Cf. Bolingbroke's letter to Swift, *Correspondence*, ed. F. E. Ball, London 1910-14, iii, 259.

173 During these years Georgia was claimed by the Spaniards, who had settled in Florida. For details see Kenneth Coleman (ed.) *A History of Georgia*, Athens, Georgia 1977, chap. 3 and Phinizy Spalding, *Oglethorpe in America*, Chicago 1977, chap. 7.

174 Seats: a place to settle; Lat. *sedes*.
Explore: search out.

176-8: Line 177 is justly admired for its massive weight. It must be granted, however, that the logic of the verses is untidy. The sense should be 'worth rises slowly everywhere, but more slowly here'; but in J.'s syntax 'ev'ry where' goes with 'confess'd', not with 'rises'.

179-81 If you want a great man to notice you, you must bribe his servant; cf. Juv. 184-9.
Retails: retail: 'to sell at second hand', Dict.

182ff. Juv.'s mention of Ucalegon (199), a figure taken from *Aeneid* 2.312, led J. to Virgil's description of burning Troy. As the cries of the crowd woke Aeneas in his palace, so J.'s sleeper is roused from his dream of a palace. Dryden's translation of the passage begins thus:

> Now peals of shouts came thundering from afar,
> Cries, threats, and loud laments, and mingled war:
> The noise approaches, though our palace stood
> Aloof from streets, encompassed with a wood.
> Louder, and yet more loud, I hear the alarms
> Of human cries, distinct, and clashing arms.
> Fear broke my slumbers.   (397-403)

187 Tremendous: terrifying.

189 Little ALL: an abridgement of Juv. 208-9.

190 Another epic expansion of Juv., recalling the fate of Aeneas after the fall of Troy.

192-3 These lines show how J. could use scholars' lumber to construct a fine couplet. 'In vain' comes from *frustra*, which was wrongly admitted into the text of Juv. 210 by certain editors and was mentioned as a variant by others. J. rightly read *frusta* (scraps); *frustra*, being a spondee, is metrically impossible.

194 Orgilio: see on 208 below.

197 Pacify: appease.

198 Servile: 'venal', the reading of the 1st ed., appeared again in 1787.

199 The line parodies the false rhetoric of the laureate tribe.

201 They give him the equivalent of the wealth he has lost – wealth which he had ‹acquired by exploiting the country's poor.

203 Dome: building.

204 Certain small boroughs ('pocket boroughs') were virtually the property, for electoral purposes of wealthy aristocrats who could sell or give the representation to men of

their choice. In addition, the ownership of a manor often carried with it the right
(called 'advowson') to appoint a clergyman to the local church. 'Restoring the price'
means giving back to the landowner enough money to purchase new estates. So
the line as a whole refers to the corrupt use of land ownership to influence parliament and church.

206 Bauble: 'a thing of more show than use', Dict.

208 Orgilio: the draft had 'Sejano'. In the mind of the reading public there was a chain
of association connecting Verres (the evil governor of Sicily), Sejanus (the powerful
favourite of Tiberius whose fall is described in Juv. 10), Wolsey (see list), and
Walpole. The evidence from *The Craftsman* and elsewhere is presented by C.B.
Ricks, *Modern Language Notes* 73 (1958) 563-8. So it is fair to think of Orgilio,
who in v.84 is the counterpart of Juv.'s Verres, as 'a man like Walpole' and of his
palace as 'a mansion like Houghton'. For the meaning of Orgilio see note on 84.
Aspire: 'to rise, to tower', Dict. sense 3.

209 Juv., as often, is more sharp and cynical. The rich man, he says, is now suspected
with good reason of having set fire to his own house (221-2). According to Fleeman,
fire insurance became possible in 1739 – the year after the publication of *London*.

210 Park: e.g. St James's Park and Hyde Park, and fashionable pleasure-gardens like
Vauxhall and Ranelagh.

211 Thales is travelling to Wales, beyond the Severn; J. was born in Lichfield near the
Trent. Oldham (199) had
An handsom Dwelling might be had in Kent.

212 Elegant retreat: this does not contradict 'secret cell' (49), for Thales does not say
that he intends to acquire such an 'elegant retreat' for himself.

213 The M.P. is living in London, where he votes as his patron tells him.

214 Prospects: views.
Smiling: *OED* gives 'cheerful', 'agreeable to the sight'; but here it seems to
have the added connotation of 'fertile'; in fact the draft had 'fruitful'. Cf. the Lat.
laetus in the first line of Virgil's *Georgics: quid faciat laetas segetes*.

215 Dungeons: basements; see George 89-90.

216-23 This elevated, and yet tender, way of writing about rural life owes something to
Milton; see, e.g., his description of Eve in *Paradise Lost* 9.427-30:
                    . . . oft stooping to support
        Each flower of slender stalk, whose head, though gay
        Carnation, purple, azure, or speck'd with gold,
        Hung drooping unsustain'd.
One must also bear in mind the Georgic tradition, which, though it started earlier,
received its main impetus from Dryden's translation of Virgil's *Georgics*. (See J.
Chalker, *The English Georgic*, London, 1969.)
    Here Thales *wants* us to see the country in these idealized terms. Rural delights
are needed as a contrast to urban horrors. And this may well have been a contrast
which J. wished to draw at this point in his career. His *general* view of country life
was much more complex. His appreciation of it was based on a thorough knowledge
of practical details, and he was by no means blind to its harshness. (See R. W.

Ketton-Cremer, 'Johnson and the Countryside' in *Johnson, Boswell and their Circle*: Essays Presented to L. F. Powell, Oxford 1965, 65-75.)

217 **Bower**: 'an arbour; a sheltered place covered with green trees, twined and bent', Dict.

218 **Beds**: Hawkins (on J.'s authority?) changed this to 'grounds' in 1787, perhaps because 'beds' was thought to be too low. Yet 'beds' is more precise.

222 **Security**: freedom from both danger and worry.

226-9 Cf. Milton, *Paradise Lost* 1.500-502:
And when the night
Darkens the streets, then wander forth the sons
Of Belial, flown with insolence and wine.
Fop: 'a man of small understanding and much ostentation', Dict.
New commission: he has just been made an officer.

228 **Frolick**: 'gay, full of levity, full of pranks', Dict.

230 **Mischievously**: in a way involving harm, wickedly. The Dict. does not give the lighter, more playful, meaning, which seems to be a later development.

233 They prudently confine their insults to the poor. The adverbial idea of 'prudently' is rendered by an adjective, which is then transferred from 'they' to 'insults'. Both processes are common in Latin poetry.

234 **Flambeau**: a lighted torch.

235 **Train**: retinue.

232-5 Cf. Oldham (202):
Yet heated, as they are, with Youth, and Wine,
If they discern a train of Flamboes shine,
If a Great Man with his gilt Coach appear,
And a strong Guard of Foot boys in the rere,
The Rascals sneak, and shrink their Heads for fear.

237 **Balmy**: mild, soothing.

239 **Midnight murd'rer**: cf. Oldham (204) 'midnight Padders'.
Faithless: the opposite of 'trusty'.

241 **Plants**: it may be argued that the variant 'leaves', adopted in 1787, rounds off the scene with the murderer's departure; but the reader has to adjust his construction on finding that 'leaves' is a transitive verb. 'Plants', moreover, is a stronger word.

242 **Tyburn**: the place of public execution until 1783, near the present site of the Marble Arch. Hanging-days, which occurred eight times a year, were observed as public holidays. Oldham (205) had
Then fatal Carts thro Holborn seldom went,
And Tyburn with few Pilgrims was content.

243-7 J. could have said 'so many are hanged that the executioner is running out of rope', or 'so many are hanged that the fleet is running out of rope', or 'so many are hanged that there won't be enough rope for the king's convoy'. The draft, which did not originally include 244-5, suggests that J. may have intended to choose the third, and strongest, possibility, or at least to combine the first and third. In the end he tried to include all three and so blurred the effect. Juv. (310-11) did not make the same mistake.

Schemes: 'The words "project" and "scheme" were anathema to Walpole's Tory critics', Kramnick 194.

245 Ways and Means: a parliamentary term for methods of raising money.

246-7 Another political shaft. 'Tempting' makes it clear that J. is referring to the eight months which George II spent in Hanover with his mistress Mme de Wallmoden from May 1736 to January 1737. This and other visits to Hanover were greatly resented; see Williams, 40-42. (It is perhaps over-ingenious, however, to see a verbal play in 'rig' which would connect it with 'riggish' = wanton.)

248 Alfred: see list.

250 Without constraint: the absence of greed and violence made penal laws unnecessary. J.'s contemporaries read about the golden age of Alfred in Sir John Spelman's *Life of Alfred the Great*, translated and edited by Thomas Hearne, Oxford 1709.

251 Deep'd the sword: the meaning should be 'lowered the sword', which provides a suitable contrast to 'held high the . . . scale'. If this is right, J. must have not only revived an obsolete verb but also given it a new sense. (The previous sense was 'to plunge or immerse deeply', *OED* 4.) Of other suggestions 'dipp'd' is at first sight attractive, but those who have studied J.'s handwriting maintain that his 'dipp'd' would hardly have been corrupted into 'deep'd' by the printer. 'Drop'd' could have been misread and would have provided the right sense. ('Drop' = 'lower' was used in fencing; cf. 'to drop one's guard' in boxing.) In that case, however, we have to exclude the more common sense, viz. 'to let fall'. If 'deep'd' was wrong, it was allowed to stand uncorrected for a very long time. 'Sheath'd', the alteration printed by Hawkins in 1787, gives an inferior antithesis and is iconographically inept.

252 Spies: Walpole had an extensive network of spies to counteract Jacobitism. See J. H. Plumb, *Sir Robert Walpole; the King's Minister*, London 1960, index under 'Spies'. Harley also had his sources of information.

Special juries: under Walpole such juries, chosen from a panel of rich landowners, were used to secure convictions in cases of seditious libel. See Greene, 307, n.17.

257 Wilds of Kent: J. must surely have considered 'banks of Trent' as a parallel to Juv.'s reference to his native Aquinum (319). But that would have meant altering v.211, where he had substituted 'Trent' for Oldham's 'Kent'. So he followed the other course and put 'Kent' here. Since we are dealing with such a strongly explicit poet, it seems improbable that 'the wilds of Kent' was meant to suggest either Canterbury cathedral or the family home of J.'s friend Elizabeth Carter. Nor, I think, does it refer to the fact that Kent was 'deconverted' by the Danes and thus became the last bastion of paganism. The more superficial explanation, based on rhyme and on the hint from Oldham, is more likely to be true.

260 Aid: J.'s text of Juv. (322) had *adjutor* (helper). Modern editors rightly prefer *auditor* (listener). Juv. is not thought of as *composing* his satires at Aquinum; if he goes there he will be on holiday. Also, it is amusing to suggest that Juv.'s lady-satires (*saturae*) might be embarrassed if a man in heavy boots showed up at their recital. But once the satires have been personified, it makes no sense to talk of them being helped. (What are they being helped to do?) Umbricius, therefore, imagines himself as a listener, not as a co-author of satiric poems.

261 Foe to vice: Prateus' note on Juv.'s *caligatus* (322) reads: 'equipped like an energetic soldier, certainly a keen foe of vice (*acer vitiorum hostis*)'. For the satirist as a foe to vice and a friend of virtue cf. Horace, *Sat.* 2.1.70 and Pope's Imitation 119-22:

> Yes, while I live, no rich or noble knave
> Shall walk the World, in credit, to his grave.
> To VIRTUE ONLY and HER FRIENDS A FRIEND,
> The World beside may murmur, or commend.

Shade: a place of seclusion. Juv.'s 'Umbricius' might possibly suggest 'the man in search of seclusion (*umbra*)'. Certainly he has nothing to do with the haruspex mentioned by Pliny the Elder (10.6) and Tacitus (*Hist.* 1.27) and referred to by some of the older commentaries.

262 Rage: in view of 'virtue's cause' and 'exert' it probably means 'zeal' or 'ardour' rather than 'anger'. Fleeman understands it in the more specialized sense of *furor poeticus* or inspiration.

DRAFTS OF THE TWO POEMS

The drafts of *London* and *The Vanity of Human Wishes* were preserved by Boswell. They were subsequently discovered among the papers which came to light at Malahide Castle, just north of Dublin, in the 1920s and 1930s. They are now in the Hyde Collection in Somerville, New Jersey. An account of the papers is given by David Buchanan in *The Treasure of Auchinleck*, London, 1975.

[   ]: letters covered by binder or missing as a result of damage to the MS.

<*italics*>: words struck out by Johnson.

The lines of the drafts have been re-ordered so as to correspond with the final versions. The drafts are reproduced in this edition, by kind permission of Oxford University Press, from *The Poems of Samuel Johnson*, ed. D. Nichol Smith and E. L. McAdam (2nd ed., revised by J. D. Fleeman, Oxford, 1974).

DRAFT OF *LONDON* (INCOMPLETE)

[*ll.* 99–106]

Illustrious Edward! from the Realms of Day
The Land of Heroes, and of Saints Survey;   100
Nor Hope the Brit⟨ons⟩ish lineaments to trace:
                                 surly
The rustic Grandeur and the ⟨manly⟩ Grace
But sunk in thoughtless Ease, and empty Show
Behold the Warriour dwindled to a Beau,
Sense, Freedom, Piety refind away   105
Of France ⟨an⟩ the Mimic and of Spain the prey.

[148–50]
          exalt each
⟨Praise evry⟩ trifle, ev'ry Vice adore
His taste in Snuff his Judgement in a Whore.
Who dwell on Balbo's courtly mien, ——   150

[198–263]
[W]ith servile Grief dependent Nobles sigh
[A]nd swell with tears the prostituted Eye

With well feignd Grattitude the pension'd Band   200
[R]efund the Plunder of the beggard land
The price of Burroughs and of Souls restore
And raise his treasures higher than before
From every part the gaudy Vassals come
And croud with sudden Wealth the rising Dome   205
Now bless'd with all the baubles of the Great
The polishd Marble and the shining Plate
Sejano sees the golden Pile aspire
And hopes from Angry Heav'n another fire.   219
   Coulds thou resign the Park and Court content   20   210
For the fair banks of Severn or of Trent
The ⟨s⟩might you find some elegant Retreat
Some hireling Senatours deserted Seat,
And Stretch your Prospects oer the fruitfull land
      rents
For less than ⟨*hires*⟩ the Dungeons of the Strand.   215
There prune thy shades, support the drooping flowrs
Divide the Rivulets, and plan the Bowrs
And while thy Bed a cheap Repast afford
Despise the dainties of a venal Lord.
On⟨*by*⟩ ev'ry Bush there artless Music sings   220
There ev'ry Breeze bears health upon its wings
On all thy Hours Security shall smile
And bless thy Evening Walk, and morn[ing] To[il]
⟨*Here Life is ventur'd if the Streets You roam*⟩
Prepare for Death, if here the Streets You roam
   sign
And make will before you sup from home   225
So Some fiery Fop, with new Commission vain
Who sleeps on brambles till he kils his Man
                   a
Some Gamesome Drunkard reeling from a Fe͟st
Provoke [a] broil, and stabs you for a jest.
Yet ev'n th[es]e Heroes mischievously gay   230
Lords of th[e] Street and terrours of the way
Flushed as they are, with Youth confu[se]d with w[ine]
Their prudent insults to the poor co[nf]ine

Mark from Afar
⟨*Afar they*⟩ mark the Flambeaus bright approach,
And Shun the shining ⟨*Co*⟩Trains and Golden Coach.   235

In vain these dangers past, your Doors you close,
And hope the Balmy blessings of repose
Cruel with guilt, and daring with despair,   248
The midnight Murd'rer burst the faithless bar,
Invades the sacred Hour of silent rest,   240
And plants his Dagger in your slumbring Breast

Well may we fear, such crouds at Tyburn dye
Lest scarce the exhausted should Rope supply
    Propose Your schemes, Ye Senatorian Band
    Whose Ways and Means support a sinking Lan[d]   245
[A]nd ⟨*xxx*⟩ Ropes be wanting in the tempting Spring
[To] rig another convoy for the King.
    A single Jayl, in Alfred's golden reign
[Cou]ld half the Nations Criminals contain
Fair Justice then without constraint adord   250
Sustain'd the Ballance, but resign'd the Sword
No⟨*r*⟩ Bribes were paid, no Special Juries known
Blest Age! but, ah! how diffrent from our own.
Much could I add—But seet the Boat at hand—   260
The tide retiring calls me from the Land   255
Farewell—When Youth, and Health and Fortu[ne] spent
You fly for refuge to the Wilds of Kent
And tir'd like me with Follies and with Crimes
        angry numbers
In ⟨*useful Satire*⟩ warn succeeding times
Then shall thy Friend, nor thou refuse his aid   260
Still foe to Vice, forsake his Cambrian Shade
In Virtue's Cause once more exert his Rage
Thy Satire point and animate thy Page.

THE VANITY OF HUMAN WISHES

[1]   Let Observation with extensive view,
Survey mankind, from China to Peru;
Remark each anxious toil, each eager strife,
And watch the busy scenes of crowded life;
Then say how hope and fear, desire and hate,
O'erspread with snares the clouded maze of fate,
Where wav'ring man, betray'd by vent'rous pride,
To tread the dreary paths without a guide,
As treach'rous phantoms in the mist delude,
Shuns fancied ills, or chases airy good;   10
How rarely Reason guides the stubborn choice,
Rules the bold hand, or prompts the suppliant voice;
How nations sink, by darling schemes oppress'd,
When Vengeance listens to the fool's request.
Fate wings with ev'ry wish th' afflictive dart,
Each gift of nature, and each grace of art,
With fatal heat impetuous courage glows,
With fatal sweetness elocution flows,
Impeachment stops the speaker's pow'rful breath,
And restless fire precipitates on death.   20
    But scarce observ'd, the knowing and the bold
Fall in the gen'ral massacre of gold;
Wide-wasting pest! that rages unconfin'd,
And crowds with crimes the records of mankind;
For gold his sword the hireling ruffian draws,
For gold the hireling judge distorts the laws;
Wealth heap'd on wealth, nor truth nor safety buys,
The dangers gather as the treasures rise.
    Let hist'ry tell where rival kings command,
And dubious title shakes the madded land,   30
When statutes glean the refuse of the sword,
How much more safe the vassal than the lord;
Low skulks the hind beneath the rage of pow'r,

And leaves the wealthy traytor in the Tow'r,
Untouch'd his cottage, and his slumbers sound,
Tho' confiscation's vulturs hover round.
The needy traveller, serene and gay,
Walks the wild heath, and sings his toil away.
Does envy seize thee? Crush th'upbraiding joy,
Increase his riches and his peace destroy;   40
New fears in dire vicissitude invade,
The rustling brake alarms, and quiv'ring shade,
Nor light nor darkness bring his pain relief,
One shews the plunder, and one hides the thief.
Yet still one gen'ral cry the skies assails,
And gain and grandeur load the tainted gales;
Few know the toiling statesman's fear or care,
Th'insidious rival and the gaping heir.
Once more, Democritus, arise on earth,
With chearful wisdom and instructive mirth,   50
See motley life in modern trappings dress'd,
And feed with varied fools th'eternal jest:
Thou who couldst laugh where want enchain'd caprice,
Toil crush'd conceit, and man was of a piece;
Where wealth unlov'd without a mourner dy'd,
And scarce a sycophant was fed by pride;
Where ne'er was known the form of mock debate,
Or seen a new-made mayor's unwieldy state;
Where change of fav'rites made no change of laws,
And senates heard before they judg'd a cause;   60
How wouldst thou shake at Britain's modish tribe,
Dart the quick taunt, and edge the piercing gibe!
Attentive truth and nature to descry,
And pierce each scene with philosophic eye.
To thee were solemn toys or empty shew,
The robes of pleasure and the veils of woe:
All aid the farce, and all thy mirth maintain,
Whose joys are causeless, or whose griefs are vain.
Such was the scorn that fill'd the sage's mind,
Renew'd at ev'ry glance on humankind;   70
How just that scorn ere yet thy voice declare,
Search every state, and canvass ev'ry pray'r.

[54]   Unnumber'd suppliants crowd Preferment's gate,
Athirst for wealth, and burning to be great;

Delusive Fortune hears th' incessant call,
They mount, they shine, evaporate, and fall.
On ev'ry stage the foes of peace attend,
Hate dogs their flight, and insult mocks their end.
Love ends with hope, the sinking statesman's door
Pours in the morning worshiper no more;   80
For growing names the weekly scribbler lies,
To growing wealth the dedicator flies,
From every room descends the painted face,
That hung the bright Palladium of the place,
And smoak'd in kitchens, or in auctions sold,
To better features yields the frame of gold;
For now no more we trace in ev'ry line
Heroic worth, benevolence divine:
The form distorted justifies the fall,
And detestation rids th' indignant wall.   90
    But will not Britain hear the last appeal,
Sign her foe's doom, or guard her fav'rite's zeal?
Through Freedom's sons no more remonstrance rings,
Degrading nobles and controuling kings;
Our supple tribes repress their patriot throats,
And ask no questions but the price of votes;
With weekly libels and septennial ale,
Their wish is full to riot and to rail.
    In full-blown dignity, see Wolsey stand,
Law in his voice, and fortune in his hand: 100
To him the church, the realm, their pow'rs consign,
Thro' him the rays of regal bounty shine;
Still to new heights his restless wishes tow'r,
Claim leads to claim, and pow'r advances pow'r;
Till conquest unresisted ceas'd to please,
And rights submitted left him none to seize.
At length his sov'reign frowns – the train of state
Mark the keen glance, and watch the sign to hate.   110
Where-e'er he turns he meets a stranger's eye,
His suppliants scorn him, and his followers fly;
At once is lost the pride of aweful state,
The golden canopy, the glitt'ring plate,
The regal palace, the luxurious board,
The liv'ried army, and the menial lord.
With age, with cares, with maladies oppress'd,
He seeks the refuge of monastic rest.

Grief aids disease, remember'd folly stings,
And his last sighs reproach the faith of kings.   120
    Speak thou, whose thoughts at humble peace repine,
Shall Wolsey's wealth, with Wolsey's end be thine?
Or liv'st thou now, with safer pride content,
The wisest justice on the banks of Trent?
For why did Wolsey near the steeps of fate,
On weak foundations raise th' enormous weight?
Why but to sink beneath misfortune's blow,
With louder ruin to the gulphs below?
    What gave great Villiers to th' assassin's knife,
And fixed disease on Harley's closing life?   130
What murder'd Wentworth, and what exil'd Hyde,
By kings protected, and to kings ally'd?
What but their wish indulg'd in courts to shine,
And pow'r too great to keep, or to resign?

[114]   When first the college rolls receive his name,
The young enthusiast quits his ease for fame;
Through all his veins the fever of renown
Burns from the strong contagion of the gown;
O'er Bodley's dome his future labours spread,
And Bacon's mansion trembles o'er his head.   140
Are these thy views? Proceed, illustrious youth,
And Virtue guard thee to the throne of Truth!
Yet should thy soul indulge the gen'rous heat,
Till captive Science yields her last retreat;
Should Reason guide thee with her brightest ray,
And pour on misty Doubt resistless day;
Should no false kindness lure to loose delight,
Nor praise relax, nor difficulty fright;
Should tempting Novelty thy cell refrain,
And Sloth effuse her opiate fumes in vain;   150
Should Beauty blunt on fops her fatal dart,
Nor claim the triumph of a letter'd heart;
Should no disease thy torpid veins invade,
Nor Melancholy's phantoms haunt thy shade;
Yet hope not life from grief or danger free,
Nor think the doom of man revers'd for thee:
Deign on the passing world to turn thine eyes,
And pause awhile from letters, to be wise;

There mark what ills the scholar's life assail,
Toil, envy, want, the patron, and the jail.   160
See nations slowly wise, and meanly just,
To buried merit raise the tardy bust.
If dreams yet flatter, once again attend,
Hear Lydiat's life, and Galileo's end.
　　Nor deem, when Learning her last prize bestows,
The glitt'ring eminence exempt from foes;
See when the vulgar 'scape, despis'd or aw'd,
Rebellion's vengeful talons seize on Laud.
From meaner minds, tho' smaller fines content,
The plunder'd palace or sequester'd rent;   170
Mark'd out by dangerous parts he meets the shock,
And fatal Learning leads him to the block:
Around his tomb let Art and Genius weep,
But hear his death, ye blockheads, hear and sleep.

[133]　　The festal blazes, the triumphal show,
The ravish'd standard, and the captive foe,
The senate's thanks, the gazette's pompous tale,
With force resistless o'er the brave prevail.
Such bribes the rapid Greek o'er Asia whirl'd,
For such the steady Romans shook the world;   180
For such in distant lands the Britons shine,
And stain with blood the Danube or the Rhine;
This pow'r has praise, that virtue scarce can warm,
Till fame supplies the universal charm.
Yet Reason frowns on war's unequal game,
Where wasted nations raise a single name,
And mortgag'd states their grandsires' wreaths regret,
From age to age in everlasting debt;
Wreaths which at last the dear-bought right convey
To rust on medals, or on stones decay.   190
　　On what foundation stands the warrior's pride,
How just his hopes let Swedish Charles decide;
A frame of adamant, a soul of fire,
No dangers fright him, and no labours tire;
O'er love, o'er fear extends his wide domain,
Unconquer'd lord of pleasure and of pain;
No joys to him pacific scepters yield,
War sounds the trump, he rushes to the field;

Behold surrounding kings their pow'r combine,
And one capitulate, and one resign;   200
Peace courts his hand, but spreads her charms in vain;
Think nothing gain'd,' he cries, 'till nought remain,
On Moscow's walls till Gothic standards fly,
And all be mine beneath the polar sky.'
The march begins in military state,
And nations on his eye suspended wait;
Stern Famine guards the solitary coast,
And Winter barricades the realms of Frost;
He comes, not want and cold his course delay;
Hide, blushing Glory, hide Pultowa's day: 210
The vanquish'd hero leaves his broken bands,
And shews his miseries in distant lands;
Condemn'd a needy supplicant to wait,
While ladies interpose, and slaves debate.
But did not Chance at length her error mend?
Did no subverted empire mark his end?
Did rival monarchs give the fatal wound?
Or hostile millions press him to the ground?
His fall was destin'd to a barren strand,
A petty fortress, and a dubious hand;   220
He left the name, at which the world grew pale,
To point a moral, or adorn a tale.

  All times their scenes of pompous woes afford,
From Persia's tyrant to Bavaria's lord.
In gay hostility, and barb'rous pride,
With half mankind embattled at his side,
Great Xerxes comes to seize the certain prey,
And starves exhausted regions in his way;
Attendant Flatt'ry counts his myriads o'er,
Till counted myriads sooth his pride no more;   230
Fresh praise is try'd till madness fires his mind,
The waves he lashes, and enchains the wind;
New pow'rs are claim'd, new pow'rs are still bestow'd,
Till rude Resistance lops the spreading god;
The daring Greeks deride the martial show,
And heap their vallies with the gaudy foe;
Th' insulted sea with humbler thoughts he gains,
A single skiff to speed his flight remains;
Th' incumber'd oar scarce leaves the dreaded coast

Through purple billows and a floating host.   240
    The bold Bavarian, in a luckless hour,
Tries the dread summits of Cesarean pow'r,
With unexpected legions bursts away,
And sees defenceless realms receive his sway;
Short sway! Fair Austria spreads her mournful charms,
The queen, the beauty, sets the world in arms;
From hill to hill the beacons rousing blaze
Spreads wide the hope of plunder and of praise;
The fierce Croatian, and the wild Hussar,
And all the sons of Ravage crowd the war;   250
The baffled prince in honour's flatt'ring bloom
Of hasty greatness finds the fatal doom,
His foes' derision, and his subjects' blame,
And steals to death from anguish and from shame.

[188]   Enlarge my life with multitude of days,
In health, in sickness, thus the suppliant prays;
Hides from himself his state, and shuns to know
That life protracted is protracted woe.
Time hovers o'er, impatient to destroy,
And shuts up all the passages of joy: 260
In vain their gifts the bounteous seasons pour,
The fruit autumnal, and the vernal flow'r,
With listless eyes the dotard views the store,
He views, and wonders that they please no more;
Now pall the tasteless meats and joyless wines,
And Luxury with sighs her slave resigns.
Approach, ye minstrels, try the soothing strain,
And yield the tuneful lenitives of pain:
No sounds alas would touch th' impervious ear,
Though dancing mountains witness'd Orpheus near;   270
Nor lute nor lyre his feeble pow'rs attend,
Nor sweeter musick of a virtuous friend,
But everlasting dictates crowd his tongue,
Perversely grave, or positively wrong.
The still returning tale, and ling'ring jest,
Perplex the fawning niece and pamper'd guest,
While growing hopes scarce awe the gath'ring sneer,
And scarce a legacy can bribe to hear;
The watchful guests still hint the last offence,

The daughter's petulance, the son's expence,   280
Improve his heady rage with treach'rous skill,
And mould his passions till they make his will.
    Unnumber'd maladies his joints invade,
Lay siege to life and press the dire blockade;
But unextinguish'd Avarice still remains,
And dreaded losses aggravate his pains;
He turns, with anxious heart and cripled hands,
His bonds of debt, and mortgages of lands;
Or views his coffers with suspicious eyes,
Unlocks his gold, and counts it till he dies.   290
    But grant, the virtues of a temp'rate prime
Bless with an age exempt from scorn or crime;
An age that melts with unperceiv'd decay,
And glides in modest innocence away;
Whose peaceful day Benevolence endears,
Whose night congratulating Conscience cheers;
The gen'ral fav'rite as the gen'ral friend:
Such age there is, and who could wish its end?
    Yet ev'n on this her load Misfortune flings,
To press the weary minutes flagging wings: 300
New sorrow rises as the day returns,
A sister sickens, or a daughter mourns.
Now kindred merit fills the sable bier,
Now lacerated friendship claims a tear.
Year chases year, decay pursues decay,
Still drops some joy from with'ring life away;
New forms arise, and diff'rent views engage,
Superfluous lags the vet'ran on the stage,
Till pitying Nature signs the last release,
And bids afflicted worth retire to peace.   310
    But few there are whom hours like these await,
Who set unclouded in the gulphs of fate.
From Lydia's monarch should the search descend,
By Solon caution'd to regard his end,
In life's last scene what prodigies surprise,
Fears of the brave, and follies of the wise!
From Marlb'rough's eyes the streams of dotage flow,
And Swift expires a driv'ler and a show.

[289]   The teeming mother, anxious for her race,
Begs for each birth the fortune of a face: 320
Yet Vane could tell what ills from beauty spring;
And Sedley curs'd the form that pleas'd a king.
Ye nymphs of rosy lips and radiant eyes,
Whom pleasure keeps too busy to be wise,
Whom joys with soft varieties invite,
By day the frolick, and the dance by night,
Who frown with vanity, who smile with art,
And ask the latest fashion of the heart,
What care, what rules your heedless charms shall save,
Each nymph your rival, and each youth your slave?   330
Against your fame with Fondness Hate combines,
The rival batters, and the lover mines.
With distant voice neglected Virtue calls,
Less heard and less, the faint remonstrance falls;
Tir'd with contempt, she quits the slipp'ry reign,
And Pride and Prudence take her seat in vain.
In crowd at once, where none the pass defend,
The harmless freedom, and the private friend.
The guardians yield, by force superior ply'd;
By Int'rest, Prudence; and by Flatt'ry, Pride.   340
Now Beauty falls betray'd, despis'd, distress'd,
And hissing Infamy proclaims the rest.

[346]   Where then shall hope and fear their objects find?
Must dull suspence corrupt the stagnant mind?
Must helpless man, in ignorance sedate,
Roll darkling down the torrent of his fate?
Must no dislike alarm, no wishes rise,
No cries attempt the mercies of the skies?
Enquirer, cease, petitions yet remain,
Which heav'n may hear, nor deem religion vain.   350
Still raise for good the supplicating voice,
But leave to heav'n the measure and the choice,
Safe in his pow'r, whose eyes discern afar
The secret ambush of a specious pray'r.
Implore his aid, in his decisions rest,
Secure whate'er he gives, he gives the best.

Yet when the sense of sacred presence fires,
And strong devotion to the skies aspires,
Pour forth thy fervours for a healthful mind,
Obedient passions, and a will resign'd;   360
For love, which scarce collective man can fill;
For patience sov'reign o'er transmuted ill;
For faith, that panting for a happier seat,
Counts death kind Nature's signal of retreat:
These goods for man the laws of heav'n ordain,
These goods he grants, who grants the pow'r to gain;
With these celestial Wisdom calms the mind,
And makes the happiness she does not find.

JUVENAL, SATIRE 10

In every land from Cadiz to the Ganges and the dawn, few can distinguish true blessings from their opposites, dispelling the mist of error. When do we have sound reasons for our fears or desires? What wish do you conceive so auspiciously that you don't regret the attempt to realise it, and its actual fulfilment? The gods before now have obligingly wrecked entire households at the request of the occupants. In peace and war alike people crave for things which prove disastrous. To many eloquence is fatal, and their own torrential fluency; one man dies from trusting in his strength and his marvellous muscles. (12) More, however, are smothered by the money which they have amassed with excessive care, and by fortunes which have outgrown all other inheritances as the British whale dwarfs the dolphin. For this reason Nero, in those terrible days, ordered a whole cohort to close Longinus' house and the great park of the over-rich Seneca, and to lay siege to the splendid mansion of the Laterani. Rarely does a soldier enter a garret. If you make a journey by night, even though you take just a few articles of plain silver, you will go in fear of sword and cudgel and tremble at the shadow of a reed swaying in the moonlight. (22) The traveller with nothing on him will sing blithely when confronted by a highwayman. As a rule the first prayer offered, and the one most familiar to every temple, is for wealth and the increase of riches, so that ours may be the biggest money-box in the whole forum. But no aconite is drunk from an earthenware mug – that's something to fear when a jewelled cup is put into your hand, or when Setine wine burns red in a broad golden bowl. Do you not approve, then, of the two philosophers, one of whom [Democritus] would laugh whenever he set foot outside the door, (30) while the opposite authority [Heraclitus] would weep? Yet anyone can manage a harsh censorious guffaw; the challenging question is 'Where did the other one get enough moisture for his eyes?' Democritus' sides would shake with incessant laughter,

JUVENAL, SATIRE 10

Omnibus in terris, quae sunt a Gadibus usque
Auroram & Gangem, pauci dignoscere possunt
Vera bona atque illis multum diversa, remota
Erroris nebula: quid enim ratione timemus
Aut cupimus? Quid tam dextro pede concipis ut te
Conatus non poeniteat votique peracti?
Evertere domos totas optantibus ipsis
Dii faciles. Nocitura toga, nocitura petuntur
Militia. Torrens dicendi copia multis
Et sua mortifera est facundia. Viribus ille   10
Confisus periit admirandisque lacertis.
Sed plures nimia congesta pecunia cura
Strangulat, & cuncta exuperans patrimonia census
Quanto delphinis balaena Britannica major.
Temporibus diris igitur jussuque Neronis
Longinum & magnos Senecae praedivitis hortos
Clausit & egregias Lateranorum obsidet aedes
Tota cohors. Rarus venit in cenacula miles.
Pauca licet portes argenti vascula puri,
Nocte iter ingressus, gladium contumque timebis   20
Et motae ad lunam trepidabis arundinis umbram.
Cantabit vacuus coram latrone viator.
Prima fere vota & cunctis notissima templis
Divitiae ut crescant, ut opes; ut maxima toto
Nostra sit arca foro. Sed nulla aconita bibuntur
Fictilibus. Tunc illa time cum pocula sumes
Gemmata, & lato Setinum ardebit in auro.
Jamne igitur laudas quod de sapientibus alter
Ridebat, quoties a limine moverat unum
Protuleratque pedem, flebat contrarius auctor?   30
Sed facilis rigidi cuivis censura cachinni.
Mirandum est unde ille oculis suffecerit humor.
Perpetuo risu pulmonem agitare solebat

even though in the cities of his time there were no purple- or scarlet-bordered togas, no fasces [ceremonial axes and rods carried by magistrates' attendants], no litters, no platforms. What if he had seen a Praetor standing up in a high car, lifted high amid the dust of the circus [i.e. the race track], dressed in the tunic of Jove and wearing a wide toga with Tyrian embroidery hanging from his shoulders and a circular crown so enormous that no neck can bear its weight – (41) in fact a public slave holds it in position, sweating; as he rides in the same chariot he also saves the great magistrate from arrogance [by reminding him that he is mortal]. Add too, the bird perched on the end of his ivory staff, the trumpeters on this side, on that the long train of dutiful clients walking in front and the white-robed citizens beside his bridle who have been transformed into friends by the dole [in lieu of dinner] thrust into their purses. Even in his day he found, wherever men gathered, material for laughter. His good sense demonstrates that men of the highest ability, destined to set a fine example, may be born in a thick climate and a country of mutton-heads [Democritus came from Abdera in S. Thrace]. (51) He used to laugh at the worries and pleasures of the mob, and sometimes at their tears, while as far as he was concerned he would tell Lady Luck to go hang herself, adding a rude gesture with his middle finger.

So these requests for which it is right to cover the knees of the gods with wax [tablets containing prayers], are either superfluous or harmful. Some men are sent hurtling down by the virulent resentment to which their power exposes them; they are destroyed by their long and impressive list of honours. Down come their statues drawn by the rope; then axe-blows smash their chariot wheels, (60) and the legs of their innocent horses are broken. Now the flames are roaring; now bellows and furnace bring a glow to the head that was worshipped by the people; the mighty Sejanus is crackling; then from the face which was number two in the whole world are made pitchers, basins, saucepans, and dishes. Put up a laurel wreath on your door, drag a big whitened bull [to ensure ritual purity] to the Capitol. Sejanus is being dragged along by a hook so that everyone can see him. Delight is universal. 'What lips he had, and what a face! Believe me, I never liked that fellow. But what charge led to his fall? Who lodged the accusation? (70) On what evidence did he prove his case? And who were the witnesses?' 'Nothing of that kind happened. A big, long-winded letter arrived from Capri [where the emperor Tiberius was living].' 'Very well – I ask no more.' But what of Remus' mob? As usual, it supports whoever wins, and abuses the condemned.

Democritus, quanquam non essent urbibus illis
Praetexta & trabeae, fasces, lectica, tribunal.
Quid si vidisset Praetorem in curribus altis
Extantem & medio sublimem in pulvere circi,
In tunica Jovis, & pictae Sarrana ferentem
Ex humeris aulaea togae, magnaeque coronae
Tantum orbem quanto cervix non sufficit ulla?   40
Quippe tenet sudans hanc publicus &, sibi Consul
Ne placeat, curru servus portatur eodem.
Da nunc & volucrem, sceptro quae surgit eburno;
Illinc cornicines, hinc praecedentia longi
Agminis officia & niveos ad fraena Quirites,
Defossa in loculis quos sportula fecit amicos.
Tunc quoque materiam risus invenit ad omnes
Occursus hominum, cujus prudentia monstrat
Summos posse viros & magna exempla daturos
Vervecum in patria crassoque sub aere nasci.   50
Ridebat curas necnon & gaudia vulgi;
Interdum et lacrymas, cum fortunae ipse minaci
Mandaret laqueum mediumque ostenderet unguem.

      Ergo supervacua haec aut perniciosa petuntur,
Propter quae fas est genua incerare deorum.
Quosdam praecipitat subjecta potentia magnae
Invidiae, mergit longa atque insignis honorum
Pagina; descendunt statuae restemque sequuntur.
Ipsas deinde rotas bigarum impacta securis
Caedit, & immeritis franguntur crura caballis.   60
Jam stridunt ignes, jam follibus atque caminis
Ardet adoratum populo caput, & crepat ingens
Sejanus: deinde ex facie toto orbe secunda
Fiunt urceoli, pelves, sartago, patellae.
Pone domi lauros, duc in Capitolia magnum
Cretatumque bovem; Sejanus ducitur unco
Spectandus: gaudent omnes: Quae labra, quis illi
Vultus erat! Nunquam, si quid mihi credis, amavi
Hunc hominem: sed quo cecidit sub crimine? Quisnam
Delator? Quibus indiciis? Quo teste probavit?   70
Nil horum. Verbosa & grandis epistola venit
A Capreis: bene habet, nil plus interrogo. Sed quid
Turba Remi? Sequitur fortunam, ut semper, & odit

If Nurscia [Etruscan goddess of Fortune] had smiled on her Tuscan favourite, if the elderly princeps [emperor] had been caught off guard and struck down, at this very moment the same public would be hailing Sejanus as Augustus. It has long abandoned care – ever since we stopped selling our votes [i.e. since the end of the free republic]. The body which once conferred commands, civil office, legions, and everything else, now restrains itself and devotes its anxious efforts to two things only: bread and games. (81) 'I hear many are to die.' 'That's certain; it's a big furnace.' 'My friend Brutidius was rather pale when I met him at the Altar of Mars. I've an awful feeling that the vanquished Ajax [i.e. Tiberius] may take his revenge for being poorly defended. Quick, let's run and stamp on Caesar's enemy as he lies on the bank. But make sure our slaves see us, so that none of them will deny it and drag his frightened master into court with his head in a noose.' These were the remarks made at the time about Sejanus; these were the furtive mutterings of the crowd. (90) Do you want to be greeted respectfully every morning, as Sejanus was; to have as many possessions; to confer on one man the Consul's chair, to put another in command of an army, to be regarded as the protector of the emperor, who is sitting on the Augustan Goats' Rock [Capri] with his herd of Chaldaean astrologers? Of course you want to have cohorts armed with spears, eminent knights, and a barrack as part of your household. Why shouldn't you? Even people who don't want to kill anyone would like the power to do so. But what is the value of prestige and prosperity if, for every joy, they bring an equal amount of sorrow? Would you sooner be wearing the bordered robe of the man who is being dragged along or (100) be a power in Fidenae or Gabii, an Aedile wearing patched clothes in empty Ulubrae, adjudicating about quantities and smashing short measures? You admit, therefore, that Sejanus didn't know what was desirable. For a man who desired excessive wealth was piling up a high tower with numerous storeys, thus ensuring that the fall would be all the greater and that once the structure had been pushed over its collapse would be devastating. What overthrew men like Crassus and Pompey and the man who tamed the citizens of Rome and brought them under the lash? [i.e. Julius Caesar]. (110) It was the pursuit of the highest position by every possible means, and the fulfilment of their grandiose prayers by gods who wished them ill. Few kings go down to Ceres' son in law [Pluto] without fatal wounds and lacerations; few tyrants fail to die a sticky death.

Damnatos: idem populus, si Nurscia Tusco
Favisset, si oppressa foret secura senectus
Principis, hac ipsa Sejanum diceret hora
Augustum. Jam pridem, ex quo suffragia nulli
Vendimus effugit curas. Nam qui dabat olim
Imperium, fasces, legiones, omnia, nunc se
Continet, atque duas tantum res anxius optat,   80
Panem & Circenses. Perituros audio multos:
Nil dubium: magna est fornacula: pallidulus mi
Brutidius meus ad Martis fuit obvius aram.
Quam timeo, victus ne poenas exigat Ajax,
Ut male defensus! Curramus praecipites &,
Dum jacet in ripa, calcemus Caesaris hostem.
Sed videant servi, ne quis neget & pavidum in jus
Cervice astricta dominum trahat. Hi sermones
Tunc de Sejano: secreta haec murmura vulgi.
Visne salutari sicut Sejanus? Habere   90
Tantumdem? Atque illi sellas donare curules,
Illum exercitibus praeponere? Tutor haberi
Principis, Augusta Caprearum in rupe sedentis
Cum grege Chaldaeo? Vis certe pila, cohortes,
Egregios equites & castra domestica. Quidni
Haec cupias? Et qui nolunt occidere quemquam
Posse volunt. Sed quae praeclara & prospera tanti,
Ut rebus laetis par sit mensura malorum?
Hujus qui trahitur praetextam sumere mavis;
An Fidenarum Gabiorumque esse potestas?   100
Et de mensura jus dicere? Vasa minora
Frangere pannosus vacuis Aedilis Ulubris?
Ergo quid optandum foret ignorasse fateris
Sejanum. Nam qui nimios optabat honores,
Et nimias poscebat opes, numerosa parabat
Excelsae turris tabulata, unde altior esset
Casus & impulsae praeceps immane ruinae.
Quid Crassos, quid Pompeios evertit & illum
Ad sua qui domitos deduxit flagra Quirites?
Summus nempe locus nulla non arte petitus,   110
Magnaque numinibus vota exaudita malignis.
Ad generum Cereris sine caede & vulnere pauci
Descendunt reges & sicca morte tyranni.

The eloquence and fame of Demosthenes and Cicero – these blessings are desired from the start, and they continue to be desired throughout the whole of Minerva's holiday, by the youngster who worships the goddess, buying her good will with at present a single coin, and who has a slave in attendance to look after his flat little satchel. But both statesmen were destroyed by their eloquence; both were brought low by the generous and abundant flood of their genius. (120) Thanks to his genius one [Cicero] had his hands and head cut off; but the public platform was never soaked with the blood of a petty advocate. 'O Rome, how fortunate! You did regenerate thanks to my consulate.' If all his utterances had been on that level he could have scorned the swords of Antony. I recommend such silly poems rather than that inspired Philippic [a speech attacking Antony], the one next to last, which everyone praises. A cruel death also snatched away the man whom Athens admired because he spoke like a rushing river and guided the full assembly with his reins [Demosthenes]. The gods frowned on his birth and fate was against him; (130) his father, whose vision was blinded by the soot of the glowing metal, sent him away from the coal and tongs and sword-bearing anvil and all Vulcan's grime to the rhetorician's school.

The trophies of war – a breastplate nailed to a mutilated tree of victory, a cheek-piece dangling from a shattered helmet, a yoke with its pole snapped off, the pennant of a disabled trireme, a dejected prisoner on the top of an arch – these are thought of as superhuman blessings. This is what excites the general, be he Greek, Roman, or foreign; this is the motive for his peril and toil. (140) So much keener is the thirst for fame than for goodness. For who embraces goodness for her own sake, if you take away the prizes? Before now countries have been ruined by a few men's greed for glory, by their passion for praise and for an inscription cut in the stones containing their ashes – stones which the rude strength of the barren fig tree manages to split (for even tombs have their mortality). Put Hannibal [i.e. his funeral urn] on the scales: how many pounds will you find in that supreme commander? This is the man who was too big for Africa, a country soaked by the Moorish ocean, reaching to the warm Nile, (150) and south to the tribes of Ethiopia and the other breed of elephants. He adds Spain to his empire; he bounds across the Pyrenees. Nature sets the snowy Alps in his path. He splits the rocks and shatters the mountains with vinegar. Now he

Eloquium ac famam Demosthenis aut Ciceronis
Incipit optare, & totis Quinquatribus optat,
Quisquis adhuc uno partam colit asse Minervam,
Quem sequitur custos angustae vernula capsae.
Eloquio sed uterque perit orator. Utrumque
Largus & exundans letho dedit ingenii fons.
Ingenio manus est & cervix caesa; nec unquam   120
Sanguine causidici maduerunt rostra pusilli.
O fortunatam natam me Consule Romam.
Antoni gladios potuit contemnere, si sic
Omnia dixisset. Ridenda poemata malo
Quam te conspicuae divina Philippica famae,
Volveris a prima quae proxima. Saevus & illum
Exitus eripuit, quem mirabantur Athenae
Torrentem & pleni moderantem fraena theatri.
Diis ille adversis genitus fatoque sinistro,
Quem pater ardentis massae fuligine lippus   130
A carbone & forcipibus gladiosque parante
Incude ac luteo Vulcano ad rhetora misit.

Bellorum exuviae, truncis affixa trophaeis
Lorica, & fracta de casside buccula pendens,
Et curtum temone jugum, victaeque triremis
Aplustre, & summo tristis captivus in arcu,
Humanis majora bonis creduntur: ad haec se
Romanus Graiusque ac barbarus induperator
Erexit: causas discriminis atque laboris
Inde habuit. Tanto major famae sitis est quam   140
Virtutis. Quis enim virtutem amplectitur ipsam,
Praemia si tollas? Patriam tamen obruit olim
Gloria paucorum, & laudis titulique cupido
Haesuri saxis cinerum custodibus; ad quae
Discutienda valent sterilis mala robora ficus:
Quandoquidem data sunt ipsis quoque fata sepulcris.
Expende Annibalem: quot libras in duce summo
Invenies? Hic est, quem non capit Africa Mauro
Perfusa Oceano Niloque admota tepenti
Rursus ad Aethiopum populos aliosque elephantos.   150
Additur imperiis Hispania: Pyrenaeum
Transilit. Opposuit natura Alpemque nivemque:
Diducit scopulos & montem rumpit aceto.

has Italy in his grasp, yet he struggles to press on further. 'Nothing is achieved,' he cries, 'unless we smash the gates with our Punic troops and I plant my standard in the middle of the Subura!' Lord, what a sight! What a picture he would have made! A one-eyed general riding on a huge Gaetulian beast [elephant]. So how did he finish up? Alas for his dreams of glory! The great man, if you please, is beaten; (160) he escapes with frantic haste into exile; and there he sits in the hall of the king's palace, an important and impressive client, waiting until it should please his Bithynian lord [King Prusias] to wake up. That soul which once turned the world upside down will meet its end, not from a sword or from stones or spears, but from something which will avenge Cannae and take reprisal for all that blood – a little ring. Go on, you maniac, dash across the wild Alps, to entertain schoolboys and become a theme for recitations! One world is not enough for the young man of Pella [Alexander]. He chafes in frustration at the narrow limits of the globe, (170) as though he were shut up on rocky Gyara or tiny Seriphus. Yet when he enters the city fortified by potters [Babylon had brick walls], he will be accommodated in a stone coffin. Death alone reveals how little human bodies are. It is believed that ships once sailed across Athos; the sea was covered with that same armada [Xerxes']; it was given a solid surface for chariot wheels. These things are believed, like all the other lies that Greece has the effrontery to put in her history books. We are assured that deep rivers ceased to run, that streams were drunk dry by the Mede as he had his lunch – all the marvels that Sostratus sings about, waving his sweaty arms. But in what condition did he return, (180) the man who would vent his savage anger with whips on the east and west winds (an outrage which they had never suffered in Aeolus' prison), the man who had bound the Earthshaker himself [Poseidon] with fetters? (It was surely a sign of softheartedness that he did not consider he deserved branding! What god would wish to serve a man like that?) But in what condition did he return? In one ship, if you please, pushing its bow slowly through blood-red waves thick with corpses. Such is the price that our much-desired glory so often demands.

'Grant me a long life, Jupiter; grant me many years!' This is the one thing you pray for, whether your complexion is healthy or pale. (190) But think of the endless and bitter afflictions that go with longevity. First, look at the face – so misshapen and hideous as to be unrecognizable; a misshapen hide instead of

Jam tenet Italiam: tamen ultra pergere tendit.
Actum, inquit, nihil est, ni Poeno milite portas
Frangimus & media vexillum pono Suburra.
O qualis facies & quali digna tabella,
Cum Gaetula ducem portaret bellua luscum!
Exitus ergo quis est? O gloria! Vincitur idem
Nempe & in exilium praeceps fugit, atque ibi magnus   160
Mirandusque cliens sedet ad praetoria regis,
Donec Bithyno libeat vigilare tyranno.
Finem animae, quae res humanas miscuit olim,
Non gladii, non saxa dabunt, non tela, sed ille
Cannarum vindex ac tanti sanguinis ultor
Annulus. I, demens, & saevas curre per Alpes,
Ut pueris placeas & declamatio fias.
Unus Pellaeo juveni non sufficit orbis:
Aestuat infelix angusto limite mundi,
Ut Gyarae clausus scopulis parvaque Seripho.   170
Cum tamen a figulis munitam intraverit urbem,
Sarcophago contentus erit. Mors sola fatetur
Quantula sint hominum corpuscula. Creditur olim
Velificatus Athos, & quidquid Graecia mendax
Audet in historia; constratum classibus iisdem
Suppositumque rotis solidum mare. Credimus altos
Defecisse amnes, epotaque flumina Medo
Prandente, & madidis cantat quae Sostratus alis.
Ille tamen qualis rediit Salamine relicta,
In Corum atque Eurum solitus saevire flagellis   180
Barbarus, Aeolio nunquam hoc in carcere passos,
Ipsum compedibus qui vinxerat Ennosigaeum?
Mitius id sane, quod non & stigmate dignum
Credidit, huic quisquam vellet servire deorum?
Sed qualis rediit? Nempe una nave cruentis
Fluctibus ac tarda per densa cadavera prora.
Has toties optata exegit gloria poenas.

Da spatium vitae, multos da Jupiter annos:
Hoc recto vultu, solum hoc & pallidus optas.
Sed quam continuis & quantis longa senectus   190
Plena malis! Deformem & tetrum ante omnia vultum
Dissimilemque sui, deformem pro cute pellem,

human flesh; baggy cheeks, and wrinkles such as an old mother ape has long had etched on her muzzle, where Thabraca [on the N. African coast] spreads its leafy glades. Young men have many individual features: A is more handsome than B and B than C; D is far more powerfully built than E; but old men all look alike – a trembling body and voice, a now hairless pate, and an infant's running nose. (200) The poor old fellow has to chew his bread with gums which have lost their cutting edge. He is repellent to his wife, his children, and himself; he even provokes the disgust of Cossus the legacy-hunter. As his palate loses its sensitivity, he no longer takes the same pleasure in food and wine; he has long since forgotten what sex was like; if you try to stimulate him, his thin tool with its enlarged vein lies limp and will remain so although it be caressed all night. What have they to look forward to, these white-haired, incapacitated loins? Moreover, one rightly regards with suspicion the kind of lust that hankers after sex without the power to achieve it. Consider now the loss of another faculty. (210) What pleasure can he get from a musician, even if he be an eminent harpist, or Seleucus or one of the other pipers who wear those fashionable mantles of gleaming gold? What difference does it make where he sits in the large theatre, when he can hardly hear the horn-players and the fanfare of trumpets? The slave announcing a visitor or telling him the time has to shout to make himself heard. Again, there's so little blood now in his chilly veins that he's only warm when he has a fever. Ailments of every kind band together and dance around his body. If you asked their names, (220) I could sooner tell you how many adulterers Hippia has loved, how many patients Themison has despatched in a single autumn, how many partners have been defrauded by Basilus, and how many wards by Hirrus, how many men are drained in a day by the tall Maura, how many schoolboys are debauched by Hamillus. I could more readily run through the country houses now owned by the fellow under whose razor my heavy young beard used to grate. One has a shoulder crippled, another his back, another his hip. This man takes food with bloodless lips from someone else's fingers; he used to bare his teeth greedily at the sight of his dinner; now he just lets his mouth fall open like a baby swallow waiting for its mother to come flying in with her beak full, going without food herself. But worse than any physical disablement is the mental

Pendentesque genas & tales aspice rugas,
Quales umbriferos ubi pandit Tabraca saltus
In vetula scalpit jam mater simia bucca.
Plurima sunt juvenum discrimina, pulcrior ille
Hoc, atque ille alio: multum hic robustior illo.
Una senum facies, cum voce trementia membra,
Et jam laeve caput, madidique infantia nasi.
Frangendus misero gingiva panis inermi.   200
Usque adeo gravis uxori natisque sibique,
Ut captatori moveat fastidia Cosso.
Non eadem vini atque cibi, torpente palato,
Gaudia. Nam coitus jam longa oblivio; vel si
Coneris, jacet exiguus cum ramice nervus,
Et quamvis tota palpetur nocte jacebit.
Anne aliquid sperare potest haec inguinis aegri
Canities? Quid quod merito suspecta libido est
Quae venerem affectat sine viribus. Aspice partis
Nunc damnum alterius. Nam quae cantante voluptas,   210
Sit licet eximius citharoedus, sitve Seleucus,
Et quibus aurata mos est fulgere lacerna?
Quid refert magni sedeat qua parte theatri,
Qui vix cornicines exaudiet atque tubarum
Concentus? Clamore opus est, ut sentiat auris,
Quem dicat venisse puer, quot nuntiet horas.
Praeterea minimus gelido jam corpore sanguis
Febre calet sola; circumsilit agmine facto
Morborum omne genus, quorum si nomina quaeras,
Promptius expediam quot amaverit Hippia moechos;   220
Quot Themison aegros autumno occiderit uno;
Quot Basilus socios, quot circumscripserit Hirrus
Pupillos; quot longa viros exorbeat uno
Maura die; quot discipulos inclinet Hamillus.
Percurram citius quot villas possideat nunc,
Quo tondente gravis juvení mihi barba sonabat.
Ille humero, hic lumbis, hic coxa debilis; ambos
Perdidit ille oculos & luscis invidet. Hujus
Pallida labra cibum capiunt digitis alienis.
Ipse ad conspectum coenae diducere rictum   230
Suetus, hiat tantum, ceu pullus hirundinis, ad quem
Ore volat pleno mater jejuna. Sed omni
Membrorum damno major dementia, quae nec

decay which fails to remember servants' names and to recognize the face of a friend with whom he has dined the previous evening, or even the children whom he has brought up. By a cruelly unfair will he forbids his own flesh and blood to be heirs; all his possessions go to Phiale. So much power has the breath of that clever mouth which was for sale for so many years in the cell of a brothel. (240) Even if his mental power remains vigorous, he must walk in front of his sons' coffins, see the pyre of his beloved wife or brother, and urns full of his sisters. These are the penalties paid by those who have been granted longevity: the woes of their house are constantly renewed; as they grow old, there are many occasions of grief; their sorrows never cease; and their dress is the black of mourning. If you can place any credence in the great Homer, the king of Pylos [Nestor], was an example of a life second only to the crow's. No doubt he is thought happy in that he evaded death for so many generations and, counting his years in hundreds, so often drank the new wine. (250) Just listen for a moment to the bitter complaints he makes about the decrees of fate and his own excessive life-span, as he watches the beard of the fierce Antilochus [his son] burning. He asks all his friends who are present why he lingers on into these times and what crime he has committed to deserve such a long life. Peleus made the same complaint as he mourned the death of Achilles; so did the other father [Laertes], for whom it, was permissible to mourn the swimming Ithacan [Ulysses]. (258) If Priam had died at some other time, when Paris had just begun to build his reckless ships, he would have gone to the shades of Assaracus [son of Tros] with Troy still standing; Cassandra and Polyxena would have rent their garments and begun the lamentation; then in a magnificent ceremony Hector and the other brothers would have carried the body on their shoulders amid the wailing of the Trojan women. So what good did his long life do him? He saw everything overturned and Asia going down in flame and steel. Then, removing his crown, the doddering old warrior took up his sword and fell to the ground before the altar of almighty Jove, like an old ox which offers its scraggy pathetic neck to the master's knife, (270) after being scorned by the ungrateful plough. His end was at least human; but the wife who survived him [Hecuba] bared her teeth and barked, having turned into a savage dog. I move quickly on to our own countrymen, passing over the king of Pontus [Mithridates], and Croesus who was told in eloquent words by the judicious Solon to pay attention to the closing laps of a long life.

Nomina servorum nec vultum agnoscit amici,
Cum quo praeterita coenavit nocte, nec illos
Quos genuit, quos eduxit. Nam codice saevo
Haeredes vetat esse suos: bona tota feruntur
Ad Phialen. Tantum artificis valet halitus oris,
Quod steterat multis in carcere fornicis annis.
Ut vigeant sensus animi, ducenda tamen sunt   240
Funera natorum, rogus aspiciendus amatae
Conjugis & fratris, plenaeque sororibus urnae.
Haec data poena diu viventibus, ut renovata
Semper clade domus multis in luctibus inque
Perpetuo maerore & nigra veste senescant.
Rex Pylius (magno si quicquam credis Homero)
Exemplum vitae fuit a cornice secundae.
Felix nimirum, qui tot per saecula mortem
Distulit atque suos jam dextra computat annos,
Quique novum toties mustum bibit: oro, parumper   250
Attendas, quantum de legibus ipse queratur
Fatorum & nimio de stamine, cum videt acris
Antilochi barbam ardentem: nam quaerit ab omni
Quisquis adest socio cur haec in tempora duret;
Quod facinus dignum tam longo admiserit aevo.
Haec eadem Peleus, raptum cum luget Achillem,
Atque alius, cui fas Ithacum lugere natantem.
Incolumi Troja Priamus venisset ad umbras
Assaraci magnis solemnibus, Hectore funus
Portante ac reliquis fratrum cervicibus, inter   260
Iliadum lacrymas, ut primos edere planctus
Cassandra inciperet, scissaque Polyxena palla,
Si foret extinctus diverso tempore, quo jam
Coeperat audaces Paris aedificare carinas.
Longa dies igitur quid contulit? Omnia vidit
Eversa, & flammis Asiam ferroque cadentem.
Tunc miles tremulus posita tulit arma tiara,
Et ruit ante aram summi Jovis, ut vetulus bos,
Qui domini cultris tenue & miserabile collum
Praebet, ab ingrato jam fastiditus aratro.   270
Exitus ille utcumque hominis: sed torva canino
Latravit rictu, quae post hunc vixerat uxor.
Festino ad nostros, & regem transeo Ponti,
Et Croesum, quem vox justi facunda Solonis

Exile, prison, the swamps of Minturnae, begging for bread in ruined
Carthage – all this resulted from [Marius'] longevity. What happier being would
nature, or indeed Rome herself, ever have borne to the world than that citizen,
(280) if, after riding before his host of prisoners and all the parade of war, he had
breathed forth his glorious soul as he prepared to step down from his Teutonic
car? Campania, with great foresight, gave a highly desirable fever to Pompey;
but the public prayers of many cities prevailed. And so Rome's fortune and his
own preserved his life – only to cut it off when he had suffered defeat. This agony
and punishment Lentulus was spared; Cethegus died without mutilation; and
Catiline fell with his corpse in one piece.

(290) When she sees the temple of Venus, the solicitous mother prays for
beauty – in a low voice for her sons, more loudly for her daughters, going to
fanciful lengths in her requests. 'Why blame me for that?' she says. 'Latona
takes pleasure in the beauty of [her daughter] Diana.' But Lucretia discourages
anyone from desiring looks like hers. Virginia would gladly have Rutila's hump
and give her own appearance to her. Moreover, a physically attractive son invariably keeps his parents in a state of wretched anxiety. For good looks and
clean living rarely go together. Even if his home rivals the austerity of the
ancient Sabines and inculcates virtuous habits, (300) even if generous nature
adds with a kindly hand the gift of an innocent character and a face which burns
with the blush of modesty (and what greater boon can nature, which is more vigi-
lant and more effective than any guardian, give to a lad?), nevertheless he is not
allowed to be a man. A seducer with big sums to spend and even bigger effrontery
has the insolence to approach the boy's own parents. Such is the confidence
placed in bribes. No despot ever castrated an *ugly* youth in his cruel castle; Nero
never violated an adolescent with bandy legs or scrofula, a pot belly or a hump
back. (310) I challenge you now to take pleasure in your son's good looks. And
worse hazards lie ahead. He will become an adulterer with indiscriminate tastes,
living in fear of all the penalties which an angry husband exacts. Nor will he have
better luck than the ill-starred Mars [who was caught in the act with Venus];

Respicere ad longae jussit spatia ultima vitae.
Exilium & carcer Minturnarumque paludes
Et mendicatus victa Carthagine panis
Hinc causas habuere. Quid illo cive tulisset
Natura in terris, quid Roma beatius unquam,
Si circumducto captivorum agmine & omni   280
Bellorum pompa, animam exhalasset opimam,
Cum de Teutonico vellet descendere curru?
Provida Pompeio dederat Campania febres
Optandas: sed multae urbes & publica vota
Vicerunt. Igitur fortuna ipsius & urbis
Servatum victo caput abstulit. Hoc cruciatu
Lentulus, hac poena caruit ceciditque Cethegus
Integer, & jacuit Catilina cadavere toto.

Formam optat modico pueris, maiore puellis
Murmure, cum Veneris fanum videt anxia mater
Usque ad delicias votorum. Cur tamen, inquit,
Corripias? Pulcra gaudet Latona Diana.
Sed vetat optari faciem Lucretia, qualem
Ipsa habuit. Cuperet Rutilae Virginia gibbum
Accipere atque suam Rutilae dare. Filius autem
Corporis egregii miseros trepidosque parentes
Semper habet. Rara est adeo concordia formae
Atque pudicitiae. Sanctos licet horrida mores
Tradiderit domus ac veteres imitata Sabinas,
Praeterea castum ingenium vultumque modestum   300
Sanguine ferventem tribuat natura benigna
Larga manu (quid enim puero conferre potest plus
Custode & cura natura potentior omni?)
Non licet esse viro: nam prodiga corruptoris
Improbitas ipsos audet tentare parentes.
Tanta in muneribus fiducia. Nullus ephebum
Deformem saeva castravit in arce tyrannus:
Nec praetextatum rapuit Nero loripedem vel
Strumosum atque utero pariter gibboque tumentem.
I nunc, et juvenis specie laetare tui, quem   310
Majora expectant discrimina. Fiet adulter
Publicus, & poenas metuet quascumque maritus
Exigit iratus: nec erit felicior astro
Martis, ut in laqueos nunquam incidat. Exigit autem

some day he too will fall into the trap. Moreover, the husband's resentment sometimes exacts more than resentment is legally allowed. One man is hacked to death
by a sword; another is cut to ribbons by a bloody whip; some adulterers even
have a mullet pushed inside them. Your young Endymion will fall for a married
lady and become her lover. (320) In due course he will do the same to a woman
for whom he cares nothing, taking Servilia's cash and stripping her of all her
jewellery. For what will any woman not do, be she a Hippia or a Catulla, to
satisfy her damp crotch? In the case of the more corrupt, that place determines
their entire behaviour. 'But if a man is clean living, what harm does he suffer
from good looks?' Well, what did Hippolytus or what did Bellerophon gain from
his strict way of life? One of the women [Phaedra] blushed with shame at the
rebuff as though she had been found unattractive, and Sthenoboea was just as
mortified as the Cretan; both whipped themselves into a fury. A woman is at her
most savage when hatred is spurred on by an injured *amour propre*. Decide what
advice you think should be given to the man [C. Silius] whom Caesar's wife
[Messalina, wife of Claudius] means to marry. (331) He is a fine fellow of ex-
cellent birth – and also extremely handsome; yet the poor man is carried away to
his death by Messalina's eyes. She has long been sitting there, all prepared in her
orange bridal veil, and a marriage bed of Tyrian purple has been made ready for
all to see in the grounds of the estate; a dowry of a million sesterces will be paid
in the old ancestral way; the priest will come, along with those who are witness-
ing the contract. Perhaps you thought all this was a secret, entrusted to just a
few? Not at all; she insists on a legal ceremony. Tell me your decision. If you
refuse to comply, you will die before lighting up time. (340) If you go through
with the crime, a short interval will elapse until the affair, which is already
known to all and sundry, reaches the Emperor's ears. He will be the last to hear
of his family's scandal. Meanwhile you obey instructions, if you think it's worth
living a few days longer. Whatever you judge to be the easier and the more
honourable course, that fine white neck must be offered to the sword.

Is there nothing, then, for which people should pray? If you want my advice,
you will leave it to the gods themselves to decide what is right for us and what
suits our circumstances. Rather than giving us what's pleasant, they will give us
what's most appropriate in each case. (350) They care more for man than he
cares for himself. We are driven by emotional impulse, a blind overpowering
desire, when we yearn for marriage and a wife who will give us children; but they
know what the wife and children are going to be like. Still, that you may have

Interdum ille dolor plus quam lex ulla dolori
Concessit. Necat hic ferro, secat ille cruentis
Verberibus, quosdam moechos & mugilis intrat.
Sed tuus Endymion dilectae fiet adulter
Matronae. Mox cum dederit Servilia nummos,
Fiet & illius quam non amat: exuet omnem   320
Corporis ornatum. Quid enim ulla negaverit udis
Inguinibus, sive est haec Hippia sive Catulla?
Deterior totos habet illic foemina mores.
Sed casto quid forma nocet? Quid profuit olim
Hippolyto grave propositum? Quid Bellerophonti?
Erubuit nempe haec ceu fastidita repulsa:
Nec Sthenoboea minus quam Cressa excanduit, & se
Concussere ambae. Mulier saevissima tunc est,
Cum stimulos odio pudor admovet. Elige quidnam
Suadendum esse putes, cui nubere Caesaris uxor   330
Destinat. Optimus hic & formosissimus idem
Gentis patriciae rapitur miser extinguendus
Messalinae oculis. Dudum sedet illa parato
Flammeolo; Tyriusque palam genialis in hortis
Sternitur & ritu decies centena dabuntur
Antiquo: veniet cum signatoribus auspex.
Haec tu secreta & paucis commissa putabas?
Non nisi legitime vult nubere. Quid placeat, dic:
Ni parere velis, pereundum est ante lucernas.
Si scelus admittas, dabitur mora parvula, dum res   340
Nota urbi & populo contingat Principis aures.
Dedecus ille domus sciet ultimus. Interea tu
Obsequere imperio, si tanti est vita dierum
Paucorum. Quicquid levius meliusque putaris,
Praebenda est gladio pulcra haec & candida cervix.

　　Nil ergo optabunt homines? Si consilium vis,
Permittes ipsis expendere numinibus quid
Conveniat nobis, rebusque sit utile nostris.
Nam pro jucundis aptissima quaeque dabunt dii.
Carior est illis homo quam sibi. Nos animorum   350
Impulsu & coeca magnaque cupidine ducti,
Conjugium petimus partumque uxoris: at illis
Notum qui pueri, qualisque futura sit uxor.
Ut tamen et poscas aliquid, voveasque sacellis

something to ask for – some reason for offering in the little chapels the holy innards and sausages of a white pigling – you should pray for a sound mind in a sound body; ask for a valiant heart which has banished the fear of death, which reckons length of days the least of nature's gifts, which is able to endure any kind of hardship, (360) is proof against anger, craves for nothing, and regards the ordeals and gruelling labours of Hercules as preferable to the sexual indulgence and dinner parties and soft cushions of Sardanapallus [an Assyrian potentate]. I'm only indicating things which you could bestow on yourself. Certainly the one way to reach a tranquil life is by the path of goodness. You really have no power, Lady Luck, if only we had the sense to see it. But we make you a goddess and give you a place in heaven.

Exta & candiduli divina tomacula porci,
Orandum est ut sit mens sana in corpore sano.
Fortem posce animum & mortis terrore carentem;
Qui spatium vitae extremum inter munera ponat
Naturae, qui ferre queat quoscumque labores;
Nesciat irasci, cupiat nihil, & potiores   360
Herculis aerumnas credat saevosque labores
Et Venere & coenis & plumis Sardanapali.
Monstro quod ipse tibi possis dare; semita certe
Tranquillae per virtutem patet unica vitae.
Nullum numen habes, si sit prudentia: sed te
Nos facimus, Fortuna, deam, coeloque locamus.

NOTE

Except for a few minor changes, the text printed above is that of the Delphin edition by L. Prateus (1684). A small number of bowdlerized passages have been supplied from a later printing of the same edition. The Delphin differs from the Oxford Classical Text at several points, of which the most important are as follows (the Delphin reading is given first):

21   *motae . . . umbram*: *mota . . . umbra*

54   *haec aut*: *aut quae*

65   *patellae*: *matellae* (chamber pots)

74   *Nurscia*: *Nortia*

78   *effugit*: *effudit* (shed)

91   *sellas*: *summas*

93   *Augusta*: *angusta* (narrow)

116   *partam*: *parcam* (thrifty)

149   *perfusa*: *percussa* (beaten)

155   *actum*: *acti*

211   *eximius citharoedus, sitve Seleucus,*: *eximius, citharoedo siue Seleuco*

263   *iam*: *non*

NOTE (cont.)

295   *atque suam*: *atque suum* obelized

313   *exigit iratus*: *irati* (obelized) *debet*

365   *sed te*: *nos te*

At v. 365 Johnson was apparently more familiar with the reading *nullum numen abest, si sit prudentia* ('No divinity is lacking if prudence be there'). 'Though I do not agree with the proverb that *nullum numen abest, si sit prudentia*, yet we may very well say that *nullum numen adest, ni sit prudentia*' ('No divinity is present if prudence be not there'). Mrs Piozzi, *Anecdotes*, 218. See *Johnsonian Miscellanies*, ed. G. B. Hill, i, 295, and Hill's note on Boswell iv, 180.

NOTES ON *THE VANITY OF HUMAN WISHES*

1-2 Does this couplet say any more than 'Let Observation with extensive observation observe mankind extensively'? As Saintsbury pointed out, observation may be broad and sweeping or minute and concentrated, and it may be directed to men or things. J. has indicated which categories are intended and, for greater concreteness, has added geographical references (*Hist. of Criticism*, 1904, vol. iii, 223, n.1).

3 Strife: 'striving' rather than 'conflict'.

5-14 The construction is: let Observation say how hope etc. o'erspread ... how rarely Reason guides ... rules ... or prompts ... how nations sink. By adding 'hope' and 'fear' to 'desire' and 'hate' (see draft) J. gave his poem a greater unity; see 343.

6 Snares: traps for the feet; Lat. *laqueus*; cf. Juv. 13.244.

7 Wav'ring: to waver = 'to totter, to be in danger of falling', Dict.
Vent'rous pride: rash arrogance.

10 Airy: lacking solidity.

11 The alteration from 'hasty' to 'stubborn' brought in the old metaphor of Reason as a charioteer. Cf. Plato, *Phaedrus* 246.

13 Darling: dearly cherished.
Schemes: see on *London* 244. One such scheme was the South Sea Bubble.

15-16 'With' governs 'gift' and 'grace' as well as 'wish'. As often, J. brings disparate elements into a unified syntactical structure: fate uses every wish (conceived by the person), each gift (conferred on him by nature) and each grace (developed by social training) to feather (i.e. direct the flight of) the arrow which brings affliction.

17-20 Note the chiastic order: courage, elocution (eloquence), speaker, fire. Thus 'fire' refers back to 'courage' and its heat.
Impeachment: a procedure whereby an accused person was prosecuted by the House of Commons before the House of Lords.
Precipitates: hurls headlong.

21 The knowing and the bold: the wise and the brave.

22 Massacre of gold: the massacre which gold carries out. J. is reproducing in English the Latin subjective genitive.

29-32 The 'where' and 'when' clauses are adverbial, but 'how much' is an indirect question, i.e. 'Let hist'ry tell how much etc.'

30 Dubious: contested.
Madded: from the transitive verb 'to mad'.

31 Tax laws destroy people who have survived war.

33 Skulks: crouches in hiding.
Hind: peasant.
Beneath the rage of power: while powerful men are raging overhead.

34 'Bonny' was changed to 'wealthy' in 1755 because the Jacobite rising of 1745 was now receding into the past. Four Scots lords were brought to the Tower of London. One (Cromarty) was pardoned; the rest (Kilmarnock, Balmerino, and Lovat) were beheaded.

38 Sings: J. has altered the meaning of Juv.'s *cantabit* (22).

39-40 Are you envious of the poor man's happiness? Does his joy make you reproach yourself? Why then, get rid of your discomfort by making him rich and miserable. The classic instance is the story of Philippus and Volteius Mena in Horace, *Epist.* 1.7.46-95; cf. *Epist.* 1.18.31.

41 New fears: not 'in contrast to old fears' but 'fears not existing before'. According to Boswell the younger, this was corrected by J. to 'now', a reading which appeared in 1787.
Dire vicissitude: terrible succession.

42-3 Brake: thicket of brambles. Understand 'alarms' again after 'shade', which here means 'shadow'.
Bring: more properly 'brings'. The slip was probably due to inadvertence; for J. altered a similar instance in v.209 when it was brought to his attention.

44 The plunder: probably the rich traveller and his valuables rather than just his valuables. This gives a slightly better balance with 'thief'. The Lat. *praeda* is similarly used.

46 Prayers for gain and grandeur taint the breezes on which they are carried upwards. For a modern reader there is something to be said for putting 'gain' and 'grandeur' in inverted commas. Immoral prayers are the subject of Persius' second satire, a poem translated by Dryden.

48 The rival and the heir are the sources, respectively, of the rich man's fear and anxiety.
Gaping: in eagerness.

49 Democritus: see list.

51 Motley: 'mingled of various colours', Dict. The word has associations with clowning.

52 The different types of buffoon which appear on the scene are the fuel which keeps the joke going.

53 In a country where poverty restricted frivolous extravagance.

54 Conceit: silly ideas.
Man was of a piece: society and manners were uniform.

55 The implication is 'nowadays rich men are loved and mourned, but those who love and mourn them are primarily interested in their wills.'

56 Sycophants obtained dinners from the proud men whom they flattered.

57 Form: 'empty show', Dict.

58 State: 'solemn pomp', Dict.

62 Dart: 'to throw offensively', Dict.

64 Philosophic: having insight combined with a true sense of values.

67 The present tenses invite us to watch Democritus' reaction as if we were his contemporaries.

71-2 Before you say how justified Democritus was, consider everyone's condition and examine his prayers.

73 Crowd Preferment's gate: Swift had said 'crowd about Preferment's gate' (*To Doctor Delany*, 93). J. has given the phrase greater energy by making 'crowd' transitive. See C. B. Ricks, *Review of English Studies* 11 (1960) 413.

76 The image is probably that of a rocket rather than of a bubble.

77 On ev'ry stage: every successful man has a stage on which he enacts his life.

80 Morning worshiper: in London, as in Rome, men called on their patron in the morning.

81 J. is referring to political weeklies. The emphasis falls on 'growing'; the unstressed 'lies' implies that journalists' distortions are taken for granted.

84 Palladium: originally the statue of Pallas Athene on which the safety of Troy depended; hence a revered image of central importance.

86 Yields: the subject is 'face' (83).

87 Line: lineament, feature.

89 The man's features are now suddenly found to be ugly, and this ugliness is said to justify his fall; cf. Juv. 67-9. The original version had 'But find the form distorted by the fall', which though witty might have suggested that the picture had fallen off the wall.

90 In our hatred we relieve the indignant wall of its burden.

91-2 Will not the people either endorse the conviction of the man as an enemy or protect him as one who has devoted himself to their interests?

93 Freedom's sons: a sarcastic reference to those who have allowed a great tradition to decay.
Remonstrance: J. has in mind the Grand Remonstrance of Dec. 1641, a document cataloguing the wrongs inflicted on the people by Charles I and presenting proposals for reform.

95 Tribes: the voting units of the Roman people, here transferred to England.

97 Libels: pamphlets; Lat. *libellus*.
Septennial ale: parliaments were elected every seven years from 1716 to 1910. The Septennial Act was defended by Walpole against its opponents in 1734. Ale was liberally provided to obtain votes.

98 They have all they need to enable them to indulge in rowdy demonstrations and abuse.

99-120 Certain details of this section recall Shakespeare, *Henry VIII*, Act 3, Scene 2.

99 Full-blown: like a flower; at the acme of his career. Cf. 353ff. of the Shakespearian passage cited above. Is 'full-blown dignity' a reminiscence of 'high-blown pride' in v.362 of the play?

100 His word was law; good fortune was his to bestow.

102 What image had J. in mind? Some think it was a stained glass window, which would, indeed, be striking if one visualizes the cardinal's red robes. But Wolsey must in some way *distribute* the rays of the king's bounty; so perhaps one should think rather of a concave lens, an instrument known to J.

103-4 The following couplet in the 1749 edition was omitted in 1755:
> Turn'd by his nod the stream of honour flows,
> His smile alone security bestows.

It is printed by Nichol Smith and McAdam, and I have retained their line-numbers for the sake of uniformity. It might have been omitted accidentally by the printer because it came at the bottom of the page from which he was copying; but it is perhaps more likely that J. discarded it so as to obtain the same total of lines as Juvenal (viz. 366). Also the image (presenting Wolsey's nod as operating a system of sluice-gates?) might have struck J. as lacking in dignity. So I have continued, with some hesitation, to follow the 1755 text.

108 Rights submitted: the submission of rights – a Latin construction, cf. *ab urbe condita*, 'from the foundation of the city'.

109 His sov'reign frowns: cf. What should this mean?
> What sudden anger's this? how have I reap'd it?
> He parted frowning from me.   *(Henry VIII* 3.2.204-6)

Train of state: retinue of courtiers.

113 At once is lost: the 1st ed. had 'Now drops at once', which was altered in view of the unfortunate sequence 'Now drops at once . . . the glittering plate'.
Pride of aweful state: the impressive appurtenances of awe-inspiring grandeur, which are enumerated in the lines that follow.

116 The menial lord: the paradox indicates the height of Wolsey's position and how it might expose him to resentment.

118 Monastic rest: after his fall, but before his arrest in 1530, Wolsey retired to Cawood Castle on the Ouse, about ten miles from York. It was the old palace of the Archbishops of York, not a monastery. Some scholars have thought that J. was referring to Leicester Abbey, where Wolsey died. But Wolsey did not seek the abbey as a place of retirement; he was merely staying there when on his way to stand trial.

120 George Cavendish (1500-61) gives the words thus: 'If I had served God as diligently as I have done the King, he would not have given me over in my grey hairs.' Cf. *Henry VIII* 3.2.456-8.

124 The wisest justice: this was the original reading, which J. altered to 'The wealthiest landlord' and then to 'The richest landlord' before returning in 1755 to his first idea. Perhaps the decision hinged on J.'s interpretation of 'safer pride' (123). Was this grandeur safer merely because it was smaller in size (in which case 'richest landlord' would have suited well enough) or because it was different in kind (the prestige of the judge depending on the fairness of his decisions rather than on his financial or political power)? In any case Juv.'s *ius dicere* (101) can hardly have been the deciding factor.

Banks of Trent: J. was thinking of Lichfield.

125-8 J. found the general shape of these lines in Dryden:

> What did the mighty Pompey's fall beget?
>
> . . . .
>
> What else but his immoderate lust for power,
> Prayers made and granted in a luckless hour?   (172-7)

125 Near the steeps of fate: the 1st ed. had 'by the steps of fate', which probably meant 'by fatal degrees' (cf. Juv.'s tower of numerous storeys in 105-6). This, however, did not prepare the reader for 'the gulphs below', since no gulphs had been mentioned. 'Near the steeps (i.e. precipice)' removed this problem, but 'steeps of fate' remains rather obscure. Perhaps it is best taken as 'the precipice of destiny'. Such a danger always awaited Wolsey, but instead of avoiding it as long as he could, he actually courted it by building an eminent and precarious career.

127 Why but to sink: as in Juv. (106) intention and result are confused – a device especially effective in a poem which maintains that our aspirations, when realised, are destructive; cf. 'wish fulfilled' in 133 below.

128 Ruin: not 'destruction', but 'fall'; Lat. *ruina*.

129-31 For the names see list. Hyde is more usually known as Clarendon.

130 J. implies that the strains of Harley's public life led to the collapse of his health. This cannot, of course, be proved, but it was an opinion held by Harley's doctor. See A. McInnes, *Robert Harley, Puritan Politician*, London 1970, 158, and cf. 149 and 175.

132 Wentworth was protected by Charles I; Hyde's daughter married the Duke of York, later James II.

134 Pericles said 'You hold your empire now as a despotism. Some think that acquiring it was wrong; but it is perilous to let it go' (Thucydides 2.63).

136 Enthusiast: the young man has 'exalted ideas' (Dict. sense 3) but is something of a hothead (Dict. sense 2 'one of a hot imagination').

137-8 The 1st ed. read

> Resistless burns the fever of renown
> Caught from the strong contagion of the gown.

In 1755 'Resistless burns' was changed to 'Through all his veins', and 'Caught' to 'Spreads'. Of these changes the first was an improvement, but the second caused an awkward repetition in 139 ('spread'). When Boswell pointed this out, J. brought back 'burns'. See Boswell, iii, 357. In this exceptional case it seemed justifiable to depart from the 1755 reading.

The lines allude with wry humour to the shirt of Nessus. Hercules killed the centaur Nessus with an arrow dipped in the Hydra's poison. Later Deianeira sent Nessus' blood-soaked shirt to her husband Hercules, believing it to be a love charm. But the poison burnt Hercules like a fire and he eventually died in agony.

139 Bodley's dome: the Bodleian Library in Oxford (not the Radcliffe Camera). 'Dome' = building. For Bodley see list.
Future labours: he sees the books which he hopes to write spreading through the library. Another allusion to the labours of Hercules.

140 Bacon's mansion: for Bacon see list. 'Mansion' = residence or living quarters; cf. 'In my Father's house are many mansions' (John 14.2). Bacon's residence was the gatehouse at the northern end of Folly Bridge, which spanned the Thames near Pembroke College. There was a tradition that the house would collapse when a man greater than Bacon passed beneath it.

142 For the idea of Virtue watching over the student's progress compare the Gate of Virtue, dating from 1567, in Caius College Cambridge.

143 Indulge the gen'rous heat: give full rein to that noble ardour.

144 Science: knowledge.

147 False kindness: counterfeit love.

149 Novelty: the spirit of frivolous innovation.
Cell: cf. *London* 49.
Refrain: keep away from.

150 The 1st ed. followed the draft. Note the effect of 'effuse . . . fumes'.

151 On fops: i.e. not on you.

152 Triumph of a letter'd heart: victory over a learned heart. (The Lat. objective genitive.)

153 Torpid: probably proleptic, 'so that they become torpid'.

154 Melancholy: not just sadness, but a condition of pathological depression which J. knew only too well.
Shade: place of seclusion.

158 Letters: learning. The 1st ed. in fact read 'learning', but this was altered in 1755, no doubt to avoid the undesirable sequence 'learning to be wise'. As often, the inferior reading was reinstated by Hawkins in 1787.

159 There: in 'the passing world' (157).

160 Envy: others envy the scholar his reputation. J. does not mean the scholar's envy of others.
Patron: 'Commonly a wretch who supports with insolence and is paid by flattery', Dict. Lord Chesterfield accepted the *Plan* of the Dictionary and paid J. £10. Seven years later, when he heard the work was about to appear, he wrote two anonymous essays in *The World* commending it to the public. J., who felt himself to have been snubbed and neglected, wrote his proud and indignant letter to Chesterfield on 7 Feb. 1755. About the same time he altered the text of this line, which in the 1st ed. had 'Toil, envy, want, the garret, and the jail'. 'Patron' remained the reading thereafter – unfortunately, as it seems to me; for although the thrust at Chesterfield and his kind was understandable as an expression of immediate resentment, it disturbed the rhetoric of the line. 'Garret' did not draw attention to itself by a sudden

flash of sardonic wit but led smoothly to the climax of 'jail', a word with which it formed a natural pair.

161·2 The adverbs carry the stress in 161 and the adjectives in 162. Milton's bust was placed in Westminster Abbey in 1737, over sixty years after his death, and Dryden 'lay long without distinction, till the Duke of Buckingham gave him a tablet' (*Lives*, ed. G. B. Hill, i, 393; cf. iii, 261). Other examples are mentioned by Nichol Smith and McAdam.

164 Lydiat . . . Galileo: see list.

165 Last prize: a bishopric or higher.

166 Foes: the reading 'woes' appeared in 1758.

167 'scape: according to Chalmers (1816) J. first had ' 'scaped', then changed it to ' 'scapes' to conform to the other present tenses in the paragraph, and finally settled on ' 'scape' because 'vulgar' was not used as a singular. ' 'scape' was, in fact, in his draft. The larger textual implications of this point are discussed by Moody (2) 25.
Aw'd: feared; *OED* sense 4, rare and by now obsolete; an example is given from 1632. For the idea that the common people are to be feared see Juv. 4.1.153f., where we are told that the tyrant Domitian was finished as soon as he antagonized the workers. No doubt rhyme was a factor in J.'s decision. In any case the usual meaning of awed (i.e. 'frightened') does not supply a proper antithesis to 'despis'd'; nor does it give a satisfactory sense.

168 Rebellion: i.e. the Puritans.
Laud: see list.

169-71 Though in the case of less distinguished minds smaller penalties are deemed sufficient (e.g. a man's house is plundered, or the rent to which he is entitled is confiscated) Laud's conspicuous abilities exposed him to the full force of his enemies' hatred.

172 It was not, strictly, Laud's scholarship that led to his death, but rather the role he played in the affairs of church and state.

174 Blockheads: somewhat tactless in view of 172. J. hesitated over it, as the draft shows, but decided to let it stand.

175 Festal: of joyful celebration.
Blazes: in this context, which has such a strong Roman element, J. seems to have in mind the fires on the altars. Sacrifices were conducted in honour of the victorious general.

177 Gazette: stressed on the first syllable.

179 The rapid Greek: see Alexander the Great in the list. Some of Alexander's most spectacular victories resulted from his speed of movement. In mentioning him J. has taken a hint from *Graius* ('Greek') in Juv. 138.

180 Steady Romans: note how 'steady' balances 'rapid' (179) and also, paradoxically, precedes 'shook'.

181 Shine: win lustre.

182 Danube: Blenheim on the Danube, 30 miles NE of Ulm, was the scene of Marlborough's victory (with the Austrians) over the French and Bavarians in 1704. **Rhine**: Marlborough laid siege to Bonn in 1703.

183-4 Praise (i.e. glory) has this degree of power: that (Lat. *ut*) virtue on her own has difficulty in stirring men's eagerness; fame is needed to supply the magic enticement which always works. Cf. Juv. 140-42. A difficult couplet. It does not give satisfactory sense to take 'that' etc. as a relative clause, with 'pow'r' as its antecedent; for virtue does not warm power but men. The original reading in J.'s draft was 'Such power', which makes the construction clearer. One suspects that J. changed it because of the different 'such's' in 179-81 – notice his indecision in the draft.

185-6 War is unequal (i.e. *iniquus*, unjust) – a game in which whole countries are devastated to raise a single man to eminence.

187-90 'Wreaths', like 'laurels', denote victory; so the sense of the second couplet is 'At the cost of many lives and ruinous sums of money victorious generals have their names and images put on medals and monuments, which invariably decay.'
Debt: both parties were worried about the National Debt (see Robertson's index). By 1749 it has risen to over £77 million (Williams 336).

191-2 'On what foundation' and 'how just his hopes' are parallel constructions. So if they are construed as direct questions, each should have a question mark. In the 1749 ed. the first only had a question mark. In 1755 J. noticed this anomaly and ruled that both were *in*direct questions after 'decide'.
Decide: i.e. for us.

192 Swedish Charles: see Charles XII in the list.

193 'Frame' and 'soul' are objective case in apposition to 'him' (194).
Adamant: 'a stone, imagined by writers, of impenetrable hardness', Dict.

195-6 Fear: as in the draft. The 1st ed. had the inferior reading 'Force'.
Extends: intransitive.
Lord: since 'his' (195) is thought of as = 'of him', 'lord' stands in apposition to 'him'. For a rather easier case see 353.

197 Pacific rule gives him no pleasure.

199-200 Combine . . . capitulate . . . resign: infinitives in the accusative and infinitive construction after 'behold'. Frederick IV of Denmark gave up the fight in 1700 (Treaty of Travendal); Augustus II of Poland abdicated in 1706 (Treaty of Altranstädt).

201 Spreads: displays.

202 Till nought remain (to be done): Juv.'s *actum nihil est* (155) reminded J. of Lucan's words about Julius Caesar:

nil actum credens, dum quid superesset agendum

De Bello Civili 2.657

Thinking nothing to have been done, as long as something remained to be done.

203-4 Contrast J.'s magnificence with the deliberate bathos of Juv. 156.

203 Gothic: according to a very old tradition, represented by Jordanes' *De Rebus Geticis* (6th cent. A.D.), the Goths came originally from Sweden under the leadership of King Berig.

209 The earlier reading 'nor . . . nor' properly required 'delays', which would have destroyed the rhyme. When J. realised this he changed 'nor . . . nor' to the more awkward 'not . . . and'.

210 Pultowa: in June 1709 Charles suffered a disastrous defeat at the hands of Peter the Great at Pultowa in the Ukraine, about 80 miles WSW of Kharkov.

212ff. Charles found refuge at Bender on the Dniester, about 40 miles SE of Kishinev. The area was at that time in Turkish hands. J. has telescoped events so as to dramatize the hero's fall; he has also exaggerated the helplessness and humiliation of Charles. In both respects he is following Juv.'s example.

214 Ladies interpose: there is some evidence that Catherine the Great, Peter's wife, helped to formulate the terms of the Treaty of Prut (1711), by which Charles was allowed to return to Sweden without Russian opposition. He did not leave, however until 1714.

216 Was he not killed while overthrowing a great power? The unexpected answer is 'no'.

220 Fortress: Frederiksten, above Frederickshald, in Norway, about 50 miles S of Oslo.
Dubious hand: there was a rumour that the bullet which killed Charles came from his own side. The matter is still debated by historians.

221f. He left the name . . . to point a moral: another combination of purpose and result.
At which the world (once) grew pale.

222 He will be remembered only as an *exemplum* of reckless ambition. Hannibal's fate is even less dignified – see Juv. 167.

223 Pompous woes: woes afflicting men in high and splendid positions. 'Pompous' (Lat. *pompa*, a ceremonial procession) did not have connotations of the ridiculous as it often has today.

224 Persia's tyrant: Xerxes (see list). At several points in what follows J. draws, not on Juv., but on Herodotus.
Bavaria's lord: Charles Albert (see list).

225 The line has both a visual and an emotional force. Xerxes, like his army, is dressed in a colourful and ostentatious style, cf. 235-6. (Herodotus describes the various uniforms at some length in 7.61ff.) He is also in high good humour, bellicose and arrogant, as one would expect from an oriental tyrant.

226 Embattled: arrayed for war.

228 Herodotus (7.118ff.) speaks of the ruinous cost of feeding Xerxes' army. J. is referring to this rather than to the story (repeated in Juv. 177) that his army drank various rivers dry (Herodotus 7.21, 43, 127 etc.).

229 Myriads: in general, vast numbers; more specifically, groups of 10,000; cf. Herodotus 7.81-3.

232 When Xerxes' bridge over the Hellespont was destroyed by a storm, he ordered the sea to be given three hundred lashes, and a pair of fetters to be thrown into the water (Herodotus 7.35). Unlike Juv., Herodotus says nothing about the punishment of the winds – a punishment which struck J. as an apt illustration of arrogant futility; see *Adventurer* 137 (26 Feb. 1754) and Preface to the Dict. para. 85.

234 Rude: the Greeks are represented as rough fellows, unimpressed by Xerxes' power and ostentation. Cf. Herodotus 7.102.

236 J. is thinking of Thermopylae, the pass so bravely defended by Leonidas. See Herodotus 7.206ff.

237 Insulted: see 232.

238-40 Xerxes' fleet was heavily defeated at Salamis in 480 B.C.; see Herodotus 8.83-96.

239f. According to Mrs Piozzi, as reported by Mrs Rose, J. once said that of all the poetry he had written this was his favourite couplet. See J. W. Croker's ed. of Boswell's *Life of Johnson* (1831) v.414.
Purple: Lat. *purpureus*, which was closer to crimson.

241 The bold Bavarian: see Charles Albert in list.

245-50 Queen Maria Theresa (see list) used her beauty and her histrionic powers to rally her peoples. She appeared in mourning before the Hungarian Diet in Pressburg on 11 Sept. 1741 and made an emotional speech ending in tears. Ten days later she had her infant son brought into the assembly. As a result the Hungarians voted a levy of 20,000 foot and over 14,000 cavalry.

245 Spreads: displays.

249f. The Croatians and Hungarians formed part of the Habsburg empire.
Hussar: a Hungarian light cavalryman. Some detachments of the levy mentioned above were ill equipped and poorly disciplined; see G. E. Rothenburg, *Notes and Queries* 209 (1964) 296-8.

250 And: Hawkins read 'With' in 1787. The purpose of the change was, presumably, to avoid the repetition of 'and'. But we do not know what authority Hawkins had; and in any case the reading was no improvement, for it made it less clear that the Croatian and the Hussar were included in 'the sons of Ravage'.

251 In honour's ... bloom: at the acme of his glory.
Flattering: concealing the precarious nature of that glory.

252 The doom which awaits power too quickly acquired.

253 'Derision' and 'blame' are in apposition to 'prince' (251).

255ff. 'I remember one day, in a conversation upon the miseries of old age, a gentleman in company observed he always thought Juvenal's description of them to be rather highly coloured, upon which the Doctor replied "No Sir – I believe not; they may not all belong to an individual, but they are collectively true of old age." Then, rolling about his head, as if snuffing up his recollection, he suddenly broke out *ille humero . . . senescant'* (Juv. 227-45). G. Kearsley in *Johnsonian Miscellanies,* ed. G. B. Hill, Oxford 1897, vol. ii, 166-7.

260 Passages of joy: the senses.

263 Store: abundance.

266 Luxury: sensual pleasure (*luxuria*), personified in Persius 5.142 – a satire about moral slavery.

268 And yield: i.e. 'produce'. Hawkins (1787) and Boswell the younger have 'Diffuse'. Perhaps this is a case where later thoughts were better; cf. the sound sequence in v.150. *Contra* Moody (2)26.
Lenitives of pain: In Horace, *Odes* 1.32.14-15, the lyre is addressed as *laborum dulce lenimen* 'sweet balm of pain'; cf. 'lyre' in 271 below.

270 Orpheus: see list.

271 Attend: listen to.

273f. The old man lays down the law about everything. His assertions are grave when gravity is not called for, and he is dogmatic even when in the wrong.

276 Perplex: not 'puzzle', but 'vex'.

277 Awe: keep in check.

279 Still hint: continually mention.

280 Petulance: not 'ill temper', but 'wantonness' or 'immodesty'.
Expence: extravagance.

281 Improve: increase.
Heady: violent.

282 Will: the pun carries the point of the line.

283 His joints: the 1st ed. read 'each Joint'.

291-2 But grant that, as a result of living temperately in one's prime, one is blessed with a respected and secure old age. According to Mrs Piozzi, formerly Mrs Thrale, J. had his mother in mind; see *Anecdotes of the Late Samuel Johnson, LL.D.,* 1786, 8.

293 In: changed to 'with' by Hawkins, 1787.

295-6 The old person's kindness makes his days peaceful and pleasant; his clear conscience makes his nights serene.

298 Could: changed to 'shall' by Hawkins, 1787.

303 Kindred merit: worthy relatives. Contrast the tone of Juv.'s phrase *plenaeque sororibus urnae* (242): 'urns full of his sisters'. 'Kindred' was prompted by Dryden:
> He numbers all his kindred in their urns (382).

304 Lacerated: torn asunder by death.

305-6 The immediate debt is to Pope's Imitation of Horace, *Epist.* 2.2.72-5:
Years following years steal something ev'ry day,
At last they steal us from ourselves away;
In one our frolics, one amusements end,
In one a mistress drops, in one a friend.
But this in turn recalls *Odes* 4.13.20 and *Ars Poetica* 60-61.

307 We are to think of changes in the social and political as well as in the natural landscape.

312 The end of such a life is like a cloudless sunset seen from the shore. With 'set' cf. the Lat. *decidere* as used in Horace, *Odes* 4.7.14 – a poem which J. translated in 1784:
damna tamen celeres reparant caelestia lunae:
nos ubi decidimus
quo pater Aeneas, quo Tullus dives et Ancus,
pulvis et umbra sumus.

The moons, however, quickly recoup their losses in the sky; when we set (or go down) to where rich Tullus and Ancus have gone, we are dust and shadow.
Gulphs: depths.

313 **Lydia's monarch**: Croesus (see list).
Descend: from antiquity down to the present.

314 **Solon**: see list.
Caution'd to regard his end: when Croesus asked Solon 'Who is the happiest man you have ever seen?', he was given an unexpected answer. In some irritation he said 'What of *my* happiness?' Solon replied 'I cannot answer until I hear that you have . ended your life well .... One must look to the end of every matter to see how it will turn out; for heaven has given many men a glimpse of happiness and then utterly overturned them.' Herodotus 1.30-33. The story is not in Juv.

315 **Prodigies**: phenomena contrary to natural expectation, illustrated in 316-18.

317 **Marlb'rough**: see list.

318 **Swift**: see list.
A driveller and a show: it was rumoured that Swift's servants admitted people for money to look at the great man in his dotage. This was denied by Swift's clergyman as early as 1749 (I. Ehrenpreis, *The Personality of Jonathan Swift*, New York and London 1958, repr. 1969, 127, n.2); J. does not refer to it in his *Life of Swift*, and one cannot be quite sure that he is referring to it here. He may simply mean that the helpless Swift was a sorry sight.

319 **Race**: family.

320 Cf. 'My face is my fortune, sir, she said' in the popular song 'Where are you going to, my pretty maid?' *The Oxford Dictionary of Nursery Rhymes*, ed. I. and P. Opie, Oxford 1952, 282.

321 **Vane**: see list.

322 **Sedley**: see list.

323ff. The bantering tone, reminiscent of *The Rape of the Lock*, grows more serious as the paragraph develops.

327 With vanity: there is no serious reason for their frowns; they merely desire to attract attention.

328 The latest fashion of the heart: something like 'the newest precept of coquetry'.

329 What care (bestowed by others), what rules (prescribed by moralists) will protect you, charming and negligent as you are? In view of 'heedless', 'care' can hardly mean 'carefulness'.

330-32 Hate (represented by each rival-nymph) combines with Fondness (represented by each youth-slave-lover) to overthrow her fame (i.e. her reputation).

330 After 330 the 1st ed. had
> An envious breast with certain mischief glows,
> And slaves, the maxim tells, are always foes.

These lines were probably felt to be superfluous in view of the forceful 331-2.

332 Battering (with a battering ram) and mining (i.e. digging underneath) were methods of attacking the walls of a besieged town.

335 Tired of being ignored, Virtue leaves the kingdom which is slipping from her control. Cf. the departure of Astraea in Juv. 6.19f.

336 Pride and Prudence are not adequate substitutes for Virtue, as we find in 339-40.

338 Both phrases are ironical. 'The harmless freedom': the liberties which, she fancies, can be allowed without harm. 'The private friend': the intimate 'friend' who will contribute to her downfall.

340 Int'rest: self interest.
By ... by: Hawkins read 'To ... to'.

341 Now: the 1st ed. had 'Here', an inferior reading arising from the draft's 'Her'.

343-8 These words formulate the objection of an imaginary listener.

344 Suspence: not of judgement, but of hope, fear, and other emotions; cf. Locke: 'During this suspension of any desire ... ' (*OED* under 'suspension' sense 5). At one stage J. wrote 'becalm the stagnant mind'. The passage is reminiscent of Pope, *Eloisa to Abelard*:
> For thee the Fates, severely kind, ordain
> A cool suspense from pleasure and from pain;
> Thy life a long dead calm of fixed repose;
> No pulse that riots, and no blood that glows.   (249-52)

345 Sedate: settled and resigned; it agrees, of course, with 'man'.

346 Roll ... torrent: the draft and 1st ed. had 'Swim ... current'. Perhaps 'swim' was was felt to be too active a verb and 'current' less grand that 'torrent'.
Darkling: in the dark (adverb). J. apparently thought of it as a participle from 'to darkle', a verb which he admitted he had never found. See Dict.

348 Attempt: try to obtain. Hawkins (1787) read 'invoke'.

349 Enquirer, cease: note the oracular tone.

350 Nor deem religion vain: Epicurus denied that the gods were concerned with the world and so regarded religion (at least of the conventional kind) as vain. J. rejected this position altogether. He found much to admire in Stoicism, but could derive no comfort from it since it gave no assurance of personal survival. 'Real alleviation of the loss of friends, and rational tranquillity in the prospect of our own dissolution, can be received only from the promises of him in whose hands are life and death, and from the assurance of another and better state, in which all tears will be wiped from the eyes, and the whole soul shall be filled with joy' *The Idler*, 41 (quoted by Nichol Smith and McAdam). The contrast with Juv. has been drawn in the Introduction (p. xiii)

354 Secret ambush: as often, J. is thinking in Latin terms. *Insidiae* meant both 'ambush' and 'crafty device'. It is the second meaning which J. has in mind, though he does not give it under 'ambush' in the Dict.
Of a . . . prayer: the prayer *is* the ambush; the Lat. genitive of definition, e.g. *ars regendi* 'the art of ruling'. For 'specious prayers' cf. Dryden's translation of Persius 2:
> 'Give me good fame, ye Powers, and make me just.'
> Thus much the rogue to public ears will trust.
> In private then: 'When wilt thou, mighty Jove,
> My wealthy uncle from this world remove?'   (15-18)

356 Secure: calmly sure. The etymology is *se* 'apart from' and *cura* 'anxiety'.

357-8 The 1st ed. read:
> Yet with the sense of sacred presence prest,
> When strong devotion fills thy glowing breast.

No doubt this was altered on account of the rhyme, which repeated that of the previous couplet. The revision supplies a transcendent as well as an immanent religious feeling.

361 Love whose embrace is so wide that the whole of mankind can barely fill it. This reading is indicated by the draft:
> For love whose grasp . . .

362 Endurance triumphs over sufferings, thereby transmuting them into blessings.

363 Seat: abode.

364 Counts: the 1st ed., like the draft, read 'thinks'.

366 A difficult line. The most likely sense seems to be: 'These goods are granted by God, who grants us the power to progress in spiritual happiness.' Cf. 'gain' intrans., sense 1: 'to have advantage', 'to be advanced in interest or happiness', Dict.

367-8 Celestial Wisdom: a Christianized adaptation of Horace's *caelestis sapientia* (*Epist.* 1.3.27). Happiness is seldom just waiting to be found; it is made by an attitude of mind, viz. wisdom. The prospect of 'finding' happiness is regarded somewhat more optimistically in the lines which J. contributed to Goldsmith's *The Traveller*, published 1765:
> How small, of all that human hearts endure,
> That part which laws or kings can cause or cure!
> Still to ourselves in every place consign'd,
> Our own felicity we make or find.   (429-32)

DRAFT OF
THE VANITY OF HUMAN WISHES

(For a note on the draft of *The Vanity of Human Wishes* see p. 41).

f. 1: '1' Let Observation with extensive view
O'erlook Mankind from China to Peru
⟨*eager*⟩
Explore each ⟨*restless*⟩ anxious toil each eager Strife
And all the busy Scenes of Crouded Life
       hot
Then say how ⟨*fierce*⟩ desire and raging Hate   5
Oerspred with snares the clouded Maze of Fate
Where wav'ring Man betray'd by vent'rous pride
To tread the dang'rous paths without a Guide
As treach'rous Phantoms in the mist delude
Shuns fancied ills or chases airy Good   10
How rarely Reason guides the hasty choice
Rules the bold hand or prompts the Suppliant voice
    Nations sink
How ⟨*Families*⟩ by darling Schemes opprest
When Vengeance listens to the Fools Request
Fate wings with ev'ry wish th' afflictive dart   15
        grace
Each Gift of Nature and each ⟨*charm*⟩ of art
With fatal Heat impetuous Courage glows
With fatal Sweetness Elocution flows
Impeachment Stops the Speaker's pow'rful breath
[20] And restless Enterprize impells to death.   20
     unobserv'd
f. 2: '2' But ⟨*unregarded*⟩ the Skilful and the bad
     Fall in
⟨*Amidst*⟩ the gen'ral Massacre of Gold
Widewasting Pest that rages unconfin'd
And crouds with crimes the records of mankind
     his Sword
For Gold ⟨*the Hireling*⟩ the hireling Ruffian draws   25
For Gold the Hireling Judge distorts the Laws

Wealth heapd on Wealth nor truth nor safety buys
The danger gathers as the treasures rise.
T⟨he⟩ell Hist'ry
⟨*Historians tell*⟩ tell where rival Kings command
⟨*From dubious titles*⟩
⟨*And Statutes glean*⟩ And dubious title shakes the madded   30
    Land

When Statutes glean the refuse of the Sword,
How much more safe the Vassal than the Lord   [30]
Low Sculks the Hind beneath the rage of Pow'r
And leaves the b⟨a⟩onny Traytor in the Tow'r
Untouch'd
⟨*Secure*⟩ his Cottage, and his Slumbers sound   35
Though Confiscations Bloodhounds yelp around
    The needy Traveller secure and gay
Walks the wild Heath, and sings his toil away
Dos Envy seize thee crush th' upbraiding joy
Encrease his Riches, and his peace destroy   40
New fear⟨e⟩s in dire vicissitude invade
The Rustling Brake alarms and quiv'ring Shade   [40]
Nor light nor Darkness bring his pain relief
One shews the plunder, and one hides the thief.
                    the
Yet still the Gen'ral Cry ⟨*from on*⟩ Skies assail   45   f. 3: '3'
    And Gain and
⟨*Assails the Skies*⟩ Greatness load the tainted Gales
Few know the toiling Statesmans fear or Care
Th' insidious Rival and the gaping Heir
Once more Democritus arise on Earth
With chearf Wisdom, and instructive mirth   50
See Motley Life in modern trappings drest
                    new born
And Feed with ⟨*Change of*⟩ Fools th' eternal Jest   [50]
Thou who couldst laugh where want enchain'd Caprice
Toil crushd Conceit, and man was of a piece,
Where wealth unlov'd without a mourner dy'd   55
And scarce a sycophant could feed on pride,
Where ne'er was ⟨*heard*⟩ the form of mock debate
Or seen ⟨*the*⟩ a new made Mayor's unweeldy State
Where change of Fav'rites made no change of laws
And senates heard before they judg'd a cause   60
Where blasted Patriots never shrunk to peers

Nor annual Tax was rais'd by annual fears.   [60]
<small>How would thou shake at</small>
⟨*Evn low built towns they*⟩ Britain's modish tribe

<small>Dart the quick taunt</small>
⟨*And unexhausted laughter*⟩ and edge the piercing Gibe
Attentive Truth and Nature to descry
And pierce each scene with philosophic eye

f. 4: '4'   To thee were solemn toys or empty Shew   65
The Robes of pleasure and the veils of woe
All aid the farce and all thy mirth maintain
Whose joys are causeless, or whose Griefs are vain
        Such was the Sorn that fill'd the Sages mind
[70] Renew'd at ev'ry Glance on Humankind   70
How just that Scorn ere yet thy voice declare
Search ev'ry State and canvass ev'ry prayer.
        Unnumber'd Suppliants croud preferment's Gate
<small>Athirst for wealth</small>
⟨*All fir'd with hope*⟩ and panting to be great
Delusive Fortune hears th' incessant Call   75
They mount they shine, evaporate and fall
On evry Stage the foes of peace attend,
Hate dogs their flight, and insult mocks their End
Love ends with Hope the Sinking Statesmans door
<small>Pours in</small>
[80] ⟨*Shows pour*⟩ the morning Worshiper no more   80
        For growing names the weekly Scribler lies
<small>To</small>
⟨*For*⟩ growing wealth the Dedicator flies.
<small>Room</small>
From every ⟨*Wall*⟩ descends the painted face
<small>the bright</small>
That hung ⟨*on high*⟩ Palladium of the place
And smok'd in Kitchens or in Auctions sold   85
To better Features yields the frame of Gold

f. 5: '5'   For now no more we trace in ev'ry Line
Heroick worth Benevolence divine
But find the form distorted by the fall
<small>why should odious</small>
[90] And ⟨*hiss the Dauber*⟩ Ruin dawb the Wall.
But will not Britain Hear the last appeal
<small>Fav'rites</small>
Sign her foes doom or g[uar]d her ⟨*Patriots*⟩ zeal   90

Through Freedoms Sons no more remonstrance rings

Degrading nobles, and controling Kings
Our Supple Tribes repress their patriot throats   95
And ask no question but the price of votes
With weekly Libels, and septennial ale
Their wish is full to riot and to rail
          ⟨*State*⟩ Dignity see
     In Fullblown ⟨*Powr see mighty*⟩ Wolsey stand
Law in his Voice, and Fortune in his Hand   100 [100]
          Realm
To him the Church the ⟨*State*⟩ their pow'rs resign
Through him the Rays of royal bounty shine
Turn'd by his nod the stream of Honour flows
His Smile alone Security bestows
Still to new heights his restless wishes towr   105
Claim leads to Claim, and powr advances Powr
     Till Conquest
⟨*Till conquest*⟩ unresisted ceasd to please
And Rights Submitted left him none to seize
At length his Sovreign frowns the train of State   [110]
Mark the Keen Glance, and watch the sign to hate   110
Where'r he turns he meets a Strangers eye   f. 6.
His Supplians Scorn him, and his Followers fly
What then availd the pride of awful State
The golden Canopy the glittring plate
     regal
The ⟨*pompous*⟩ Palace—the luxurious Board   115
The livried Army, or the menial Lord
With age, with cares, with maladies opprest
He seeks the refuge of monastic rest
Grief and Disease, remember'd folly Stings
And his last words reproach the faith of Kings   120 [120]
          thoughts at humble
     Speak thou whose ₐ peace repine,
Shall Wolseys wealth, with Wolsey's end be thine
     livst thou
Or ⟨*statesmens*⟩ now with safer Pride content
     wealthiest Landlord
The ⟨*Wisest Justice*⟩ on the Bank of Trent
     ⟨*w*⟩
For why did Wolsey by the Steeps of Fate   125
On weak foundations raise th' enormous weight
Why but ⟨*th*⟩to sink beneath misfortunes blow
With louder Ruin to the Gulphs below

[What gave great Villiers to th Assassins Knife
[130] ⟨W⟩ And fix'd Disease on Harley's closing life   130
What murderd Wentworth and what exile Hyde
By Kings protected and to Kings allied

ir   indulg'd

f. 7.   What but the wish ∧ in Courts to shine
And pow'r too great to keep or to resign?
   When first the College Rolls receive his name   135
The Young Enthusiast quits his ease for fame

Quick fires his breast
⟨*Each act betrays*⟩ the fever of renown
Caught from the strong Contagion of the Gown
⟨*On Isis banks he waves, from noise withdrawn*⟩
[140] ⟨*In sober state th' imaginary Lawn*⟩
O'er Bodley's Dome his future Labours spread
And Bacon's Mansion trembles o'er his head.   140
Are these thy views, proceed illustrious Youth
And Virtue guard thee to the throne of Truth
Yet should th⟨e⟩y ⟨*fate*⟩ Soul indulge the gen'rous Heat
Till Captive Science yields her last Retreat
Should Reason guide thee with her brightest Ray   145
And pour on misty Doubt resistless day
Should no false kindness lure to loose delight
[150] Nor Praise relax, nor difficulty fright
Should tempting Novelty thy cell refrain
And Sloth's bland opiates shed their fumes in vain   150

f. 8: '3'   Should Beauty blunt on fops her fatal dart
Nor claim the triumph of a letter'd heart
⟨*SNor*⟩ Should no Disease thy torpid veins invade
Nor Melancholys Spectres haunt thy Shade

hope
Yet ⟨*dream*⟩ not Life from Grief or Danger free,   155
Nor think the doom of Man revers'd for thee

Deign   passing   to
⟨*Turn*⟩ on the ∧ world ⟨*awhil*⟩ turn thine eyes
[160] And pause awhile from Learning to be wise
There mark what ill the Scholar's life assail

the
Toil envy Want ⟨*an*⟩ Garret and the Jayl   160
   See Nations slowly wise, and meanly just,
To buried merit raise the tardy Bust.

Dreams
If ⟨*Hope*⟩ yet flatter once again attend

Hear Lydiats life and Galileo's End.
     deem when
  Nor ⟨*think though*⟩ Learning her last prize bestow   165
  e
Th⟨*at*⟩ glittering Eminence exempt from Foes
See when the Vulgar scape despis'd or aw'd
Rebellions vengeful Talons seize on Laud   [170]
From meaner minds though smaller fines content
The plundred palace or sequestred Rent   170
Mark'd out by dang'rous parts he meets the schock
And fatal Learning leads him to the Block
Around his Tomb let art and Genius weep   f. 9: '5'
But hear his death ye ⟨*Block*⟩heads, hear and sleep
  The festal Blazes, the triumphal Show   175
The ravish'd Standard, and the Captive Foe
The Senate's thanks, the Gazette's pompous tale
With force resistless o'er the Brave prevail   [180]
Such
⟨*These*⟩ Bribes the rapid Greek o'er Asia whirl'd
Such   a
For ⟨*these*⟩ the stedy Romans shook the world,   180
   such
For ⟨*these*⟩ in distant lands the Britons shine
And stain with blood the Danube or the Rhine
Such pow'er has praise that virtues scarce can ⟨*ch*⟩warm
Till Fame supplies the universal charm
Yet Reason ⟨*blush*⟩ Frowns on War's unequal Game   185
Where wasted Nations raise a single name
      their Grandsires
And mortgaged States ⟨*their former*⟩ wreaths regret
 From age to age in everlasting
⟨*Their Grandsires Glories*⟩ debt   [190]
  Wreaths which at last
⟨*Great souls whose natu*⟩ the dear bought Right convey
To Rust on Medals or on Stones decay.   190
         pride
  On what Foundation stands the Warrior's ⟨*fame*⟩
How just his Hopes let Swedish Charles decide
A frame of Adamant a soul of Fire
No dangers fright him, and no labours tire.
O'er Love o'er Fear extends his wide domain   195
Unconquer'd Lord of pleasure and of pain
No joys to him pacific Scepters yield   f. 10.
War sounds the trump he rushes to the field   [200]

In vain Surrounding Kings their pow'rs combine
See One capitulate and one resign.   200
Peace courts his Hand, her Fondness he disdains
                                   till
Think nothing gain'd, he cries ⟨th⟩ nought remains
On Moscows walls till Gothic Standards fly
And all is mine beneath the polar Sky
The march begins in military State   205
And Nations ⟨wait⟩ on his eye suspended wait
Stern Famine guards the solitary Coast
[210] And Winter barricades the realms of frost
He comes nor want nor cold his course delay
Hide blushing Glory, hide Pultowa's day   210
The vanquish'd Hero leaves his broken bands
                 shews
And ⟨hides⟩ his miseries in distant lands.
Condemn'd a needy Supplicant to wait
While Ladies interpose, and slaves debate
But did not Chance at length her errour mend   215
Did no Subverted Empire mark his end
Did rival Monarchs give the fatal wound
[220] Or Hostile Millions press him to the Ground
His Fall was destin'd to a barren Strand
               petty
A ⟨nameless⟩ Fortress, and a nameless hand   220

He left the name at which the world grew pale
To paint a moral, or adorn a tale.

All Times their Scenes of pompous Woes afford
From Persia's Tyrant to Bavaria's Lord,
In gay Hostility, and barb'rous pride   225
With half Mankind embattled on his Side
Great Xerxes comes to seize the certain prey
[230] And starves exhausted regions in his way
Attendant Flatt'ry counts his myriads o'er
Till counted Myriads sooth his pride no more   230
     Fresh
⟨New⟩ praise is tried till Madness fires his mind
The waves he lashes and enchains the wind
New Pow'rs are claimed new pow'rs are still bestow'd
Till rude resistance lops the spreading God
The daring Greeks deride the martial Shew   235
And heap their vallies with the gaudy foe

Th' insulted Sea with humbler thought he gains
A single Skiff to Speed his flight remains   [240]
Th' incumberd Oar scarce leaves the dreaded Coast
Through purple Billows and a floating Host.   240
    The bold Bavarian in a luckless hour
Tries the dread summits of Cesarean pow'r
[W]ith unexpected Legions pow'rs away
[An]d sees defenceless realms receive his sway
Short sway for Austria spreads her mournful Charms   245   f. 12.
The Queen the Beauty sets the world in arms
From hill to hill the Beacons rousing blaze
Spreads wide the hope of plunder and of praise   [250]
  fierce Croatian
The ⟨sons of Ravage⟩ and the wild Hussar
And all the son of ravage croud the war   250
The baffled Prince in honours flattring bloom
Of hasty greatness finds the hasty doom
His foes derision and his Subjects blame
And steals to Death from anguish and from Shame

    Enlarge my Life with multitude of Days   255
In health, in Sickness thus the Suppliant
Hides from himself his State and shuns to know
That Life protracted is protracted woe
Time hovers o'er impatient to destroy
And s⟨to⟩huts up all the passages of Joy   260
In vain their gifts the bounteous seasons pour

The Fruit autumnal and the vernal flowr
With listless eyes the Dotard views the store
He views and wonders why they please no more
  ⟨Th⟩ Now
⟨tasted tast⟩ pall the tastless meats and joyless wines   265
[An]d Luxury with Sighs her Slave resigns
Approach ye minstrels try the soothing Strain   f. 13.
    tuneful
And yield the ⟨soothing⟩ lenitives of pain.   [270]
The Notes unfelt would strike th' impervious ear
Though dancing Mountains witness'd Orpheus near   270
Nor lute nor Lyre his feeble pow'rs attend
Nor sweeter musick of a virtuous friend

              r
But everlasting dictates c‸oud his tongue

or
Perversely grave ⟨*and*⟩ positively wrong
The still returning tale and ling'ring Jest
⟨*Still rise the long tran*⟩
Perplex the fawning Neice and pamper'd Guest
⟨*The dull Conjecture*⟩   275
While growing hopes ⟨*re*⟩ scarce awe the gath'ring Sneer
        scarce a Legacy
And ⟨*Guests are brib'd*⟩ can bribe to hear   [290]
        watchful
The ⟨*treachrous G*⟩ Guests still hint⟨*s*⟩ the last offence
The ⟨*ruinous*⟩ Daughter's insolence the Son's expence   280
Improve his heady rage with treach'rous skill
And mould his passions till they make his will.
        Unnumberd Maladies ⟨*his*⟩ each joint invade
Lay siege to life and press the dire blockade

But unextinguish'd Av'rice still remains   285
And dreaded losses aggravate his pains
He turns with anxious heart and cripled hands
His bonds of Debt, and Mortgages of Lands
Or views his Coffers with suspicious eyes   f. 14.
Unlocks his Gold and counts it till he dies.   290
        But grant, the virtues of a temp'rate prime
Bless with an age exempt from scorn or crime
An Age that melts in unperceived decay
And glides in modest innocence away
Whose peaceful day benevolence endears   295
Whose night congratulating Conscience cheers
        gen'ral
The ⟨*common*⟩ fav'rite as the gen'ral Friend
Such Age the is, and who could wish its end   [300]

        Yet evn on this her ⟨*loa*⟩ loads Misfortune flings
        press   weary   hanging
To ⟨*loade*⟩ the ⟨*lingring*⟩ Minutes ⟨*weary*⟩ wings   300
        New Sorrow rises as the day returns
⟨*Each passing day some cause of sorrow sends*⟩
                        Daughter mourns
A Sister Sickens or a ⟨*Child offends*⟩
Now kindred merit fills the mournful Bier
Now lacerated Friendship claims a tear
Year chases Year Decay persues decay   305
Still drops some Joy from withring life away

New forms She sees whom different views engage
And lags superfluous on th' incumbred
⟨*And chearless treads the desolated*⟩ stage   [310]
Till pitying Nature signs the last release
And bids afflicted worth retire to peace   310
But few there are whom hours like these await   f. 15.
Who set unclouded in the Gulphs of Fate
    From Lydia's Monarch should the search descend
By Solon caution'd to regard his end
In Lifes last Scene what prodigies surprise   315
    Fears of the brave
⟨*The Wise man's Follies*⟩ and follies of the wise
From Marlbrough's eyes the Streams of dotage flow
And Swift expires a Driv'ler and a Show.
    The teeming Mother anxious for her race
Begs for each Birth the fortune of a face   320
Yet Vane could tell what ills from Beauty spring
And Sedley curs'd the form that pleasd a King
Ye Nymphs of rosy lips and radiant eye
Whom pleasure keeps too busy to be wise
Whom joys in soft vicissitudes invite   325
By day the frolick and the dance by night
Who frown with vanity who smile ⟨*by*⟩ with art
And ask the latest fashion of the Heart   [330]
            what rules your heedless charms shall save
What care ⟨*your charms from wretchedness*⟩
Each Nymph your rival and each youth your Slave   330
    n envious
A ⟨*Rivals*⟩ Breasts with certain Mischief glow
And slaves, the Maxim tells, are always foes.
Against your Fame with Fondness Hate combines   f. 16.
The Rival batters, and the Lover mines
With distant voice neglected Virtue calls
Less heard and less the faint Remonstrance falls
Tir'd with contempt ⟨*She at*⟩ She quits the Slippry reign 335
And Pride and Prudence take her seat in vain   [340]
            pass
In croud at once where none the ⟨*fort*⟩ defend
The harmless freedom and the private Friend
            by
The Guardians yield ⟨*with*⟩ force resistless plied
By Intrest Prudence and by Flatt'ry Pride   340

          falls betray'd despis'd distress'd
Her Beauty'⟨*s drops her pomp betray*⟩
And shout Infamy proclaims the rest   346]

   Where then shall Hope and fear their Objects find
              becalm
Must dull Suspense ⟨*still e*⟩ the stagnant Mind
Must helpless Man in ignorance sedate   345
Swim darkling down the current of his fate   [350]
Must no dislike
⟨*Enquirer cease*⟩ alarm no wishes rise
No cries attempt the mercies of the skies
⟨*Which Heavn may hear*⟩
Enquirer cease, petitions yet remain
Which Heavn may hear, nor deem Religion vain   350
For Blessing, raise the supplicating voice   f. 17.
But leave to Heavn the measure and the choice
Safe in his Pow'r whose eyes discern afar
The secret ambush of a Specious pray'r
Implore his aid, in his decisions rest,   355
And hope with humble confidence the best   [360]
Yet with the sense of sacred presence prest
   When strong
⟨*If Aspirations*⟩ Devotion fills thy glowing breast
   Pour
⟨*Breat*⟩ forth thy fervours for a ⟨*Soul re*⟩ mind
             healthful
Obedient Passions and a will resignd   360
    which scarce
For Love ⟨*whose grasp Creation*⟩ collective Man can fill,
For Patience Sov'reign o'er transmuted ill,
For Hope that panting for a happier seat
Thinks Death kind Nature's signal of Retreat
These goods for Man the laws of Heav'n ordain   365
These Goods he grants who grants the pow'r to gain   [370]
With these celestial Wisdom calms the mind
And makes the Happiness she do's not find   [372]

LIST OF NAMES

Alexander the Great (356-323 B.C.) King of Macedon. His empire stretched from the Danube to the Indus and included Egypt.

Alfred (849-899) King of Wessex, which he defended against the Danish invaders; 'father of the British navy'; lawgiver, educator, Christian gentleman.

Bacon, Roger (c.1214-c.1294) distinguished scholar, philosopher, and man of science. His work in Paris and Oxford aroused fierce opposition, and he spent many years in prison.

Bodley, Sir Thomas (1545-1613) scholar, M.P., and diplomat; he founded the Bodleian Library at Oxford, which was formally opened in 1603.

Charles XII of Sweden (1682-1718) On coming to power in 1697 he was faced with the hostile alliance of Denmark, Saxony, and Russia. He dealt successfully with the first two, but the combination of the Russian winter and the scorched earth policy proved too strong for him. As a supporter of the Old Pretender, Charles was popular with the Tories; later his career became widely known in England through Voltaire's biography (translated in 1732). He had the virtues and defects of a heroic warrior.

Charles Albert of Bavaria (1697-1745) With the support of France, Prussia, and Spain Charles Albert hoped to take over the Habsburg territories. French and Bavarian armies gained early successes in Upper Austria and Bohemia, and Charles Albert was elected Emperor in January 1742. But Prussia withdrew, having gained Silesia; England and Hanover supported Maria Theresa; and Charles Albert was soon driven from Munich, his own capital. He was restored by Frederick the Great in 1744, but died, worn out, in the following year.

Croesus (c.595-546 B.C.) King of Lydia; conquered the Greek cities of Asia Minor and amassed enormous wealth.

Democritus of Abdera (5th and early 4th cent. B.C.) a major figure in Greek thought; a pioneer of the atomic theory which was taken over by Epicurus; known in later antiquity as 'the laughing philosopher' because of his treatise 'On Cheerfulness'.

Edward III (1312-77) a king of restless energy who engaged in numerous campaigns against the Scots, the Spaniards, and the French. His most notable victory was over the French at Crécy near Abbeville in 1346.

Galileo (1564-1642) with the aid of a telescope supported Copernicus' theory that the earth revolved round the sun; clashed with the church authorities; was detained by the Inquisition in 1633 and examined under the threat of torture. He spent the last eight years of his life in enforced seclusion.

Harley, Robert (1661-1724) Earl of Oxford, an able but devious parliamentarian who rose to power under Queen Anne, forming a Tory ministry in 1710. Five years earlier he began to collect the great library which was catalogued by Johnson.

Henry V (1387-1422) became king in 1413; secured domestic peace before embarking on his French campaigns; married the French king's daughter Catherine in 1420; at home prompted church reform and encouraged commerce. A major European figure.

Hyde, Edward (1609-74) Earl of Clarendon, barrister and M.P.; councillor of Charles I and Charles II. The latter dismissed him in 1667, whereupon the Commons arraigned him for treason. Hyde took refuge in France, where he completed his 'History of the Rebellion'.

Laud, William (1573-1645) an authoritarian divine who supported the king in his struggle with the Commons; Chancellor of Oxford 1629; Archbishop of Canterbury 1633; impeached for treason in 1640 and, as a result of pressure from the Commons, beheaded in 1645.

Lydiat, Thomas (1572-1646) a divine who wrote numerous works on astronomy, mathematics, and chronology. He always had difficulty in making a living, but his worst misfortune came in 1629 (or 1630) when, unable to pay the debts contracted by his brother, he was put in prison. Laud and Ussher secured his release, but he remained in wretched circumstances and was imprisoned on two subsequent occasions before his death.

Maria Theresa (1717-80) Empress of Austria; rallied her heterogeneous peoples in 1741 against Prussia, France, and Bavaria; allied herself with France in the Seven Years War. Internally she reorganized the administration and carried out social, religious and educational reforms. An attractive portrait in E. Crankshaw, *Maria Theresa* (London 1969) facing p. 32.

Marlborough, John Churchill, First Duke (1650-1722). His victories at Blenheim (1704), Ramillies (1706), Oudenarde (1708), and Malplaquet (1709) make him one of England's greatest generals. Though handsomely rewarded for his services, he had a reputation for avarice and was suspected of prolonging the war for private gain. He suffered two strokes in 1716, and his later years were spent in decline, but he was spared the kind of collapse which overtook Swift.

Orpheus the Thracian who, according to Greek poets, could attract animals, trees, and even rocks by his song. He persuaded Pluto to allow Eurydice to return to earth, but he lost her again by looking back.

Sedley, Catherine (1657-1717) rich and witty, but by no means a beauty. Still, her form must have pleased James II, for she remained his mistress for nearly ten years and he made her Countess of Dorchester in 1686. After his fall she lived without hardship and married Sir David Colyear in 1696. Not a very cogent example of Johnson's thesis.

Solon reformed the law, constitution, and economy of early 6th century Athens and was regarded as one of the seven sages of ancient Greece. The meeting with Croesus recounted by Herodotus (1.30-33) is rejected by historians on chronological grounds.

Swift, Jonathan (1667-1745) Dean of St Patrick's Dublin; a major personality in politics; author of 'The Tale of a Tub', 'A Modest Proposal', and 'Gulliver's Travels'. In addition to other afflictions he suffered a brain lesion in 1742 which rendered him a helpless invalid for the last three years of his life.

Vane, Anne (1705-36) maid of honour to Queen Caroline and mistress of Frederick, Prince of Wales. Her three-year-old son died in February 1736 and the unfortunate mother a few weeks later.

Villiers (1), George (1592-1628) First Duke of Buckingham, favourite of James I and Charles I. His foreign policy, prosecuted with royal support against the wishes of parliament, led to disastrous failures. The assassin, John Felton, acted partly from a sense of grievance, for Buckingham had refused him a commission in the army; but he had also read the remonstrance of the Commons against Buckingham and claimed he was striking a blow for freedom.

Villiers (2), George (1628-87), Second Duke of Buckingham, a charming and many-sided man, but shallow and unreliable. At certain times in his chequered career he was very rich, but at the end of his life he was heavily in debt. The scene of squalor so memorably described by Pope, *Moral Essays*, Epistle iii, 299, is, however, non-historical.

Wentworth, Thomas (1593-1641) Earl of Strafford, chief adviser to Charles I from 1639 on; Lord Lieutenant of Ireland 1640. He was a severe and vigorous champion of the king against the Irish, the Scots, and the Commons. In the end, however, his sovereign could not save him from impeachment and execution.

Wolsey, Thomas (1475-1530) Archbishop of York 1514; created a Cardinal by Pope Leo X 1515; served Henry VIII in his foreign policy from 1512 on, acquiring great wealth and power but alienating both the Commons and the nobles. He failed to obtain from the Pope the divorce which Henry was seeking from Catherine of Aragon – largely because of the power of her nephew, the Emperor Charles V. On his fall he retired to Cawood, where he was arrested on a charge of treason. On his way to London he died at Leicester Abbey.

Xerxes I, son of Darius I King of Persia, became king in 485 B.C. In 483 he began preparations for his invasion of Greece to avenge the defeat of Darius at Marathon (490). In 480 he set out from Sardis, crossed the Hellespont, defeated the Greek fleet at Artemisium, and sacked Athens. Thanks to a stratagem of Themistocles, he attacked the Greek fleet at Salamis in September and was heavily defeated. Little is known of his later years. He was assassinated in 465 B.C.